An Autobiography

Fred ZINNEMANN

An Autobiography

A LIFE IN THE MOVIES

A ROBERT STEWART BOOK

Charles Scribner's Sons
New York

Maxwell Macmillan International
New York   Oxford   Singapore   Sydney

This book grew out of
conversations with the film critic

Alexander Walker,

to whom I wish to express
my gratitude – *F.Z.*

Charles Scribner's Sons
Macmillan Publishing Company
866 Third Avenue
New York, NY 10022

Macmillan Publishing Company is part of the Maxwell
Communication Group of Companies.

Library of Congress Cataloging-in-Publication Data

Zinnemann, Fred, 1907–
   A life in the movies: an autobiography/by Fred Zinnemann.
      p.   cm.
   "A Robert Stewart book."
   Includes index
   ISBN 0-684-19050-8
   1. Zinnemann, Fred, 1907–   .   2. Motion picture
producers and directors—United States—Biography.
I. Title.
PN1998.3Z56A3   1992
791.43′0233′092 – dc20
[B]   91–21676
                                                                  CIP

Macmillan Books are available at special discounts for
bulk purchases for sales promotions, premiums, fund-raising
or educational use. For details, contact:

Special Sales Director
Macmillan Publishing Company
866 Third Avenue
New York, NY 10022

10 9 8 7 6 5 4 3 2 1

Designed by Fielding Rowinski
Printed in Great Britain

Contents

For Renée, Tim and Stephanie

Early Days
(1907–1933)

How did I manage to become a film director?

Born in Austria in 1907, I had always dreamt of becoming a musician; but as a teenager faced with the choice of a profession, I soon found out that I had hardly any talent at all. Coming from a family of physicians, I might have tried to follow in my father's footsteps, but there was clearly no sense in it: Vienna, where I had grown up during World War One, was now the capital of a tiny, defeated, impoverished country, overflowing with young doctors without patients, who spent long hours in coffee houses studying newspapers or playing chess.

Vienna was a somber place in those early post-war years. The Allied blockade had done its work: there had been sawdust in our bread, hardly any milk, and many kids were growing up with rickets and soft bones. It was only after the Armistice in 1918 that food relief had been brought from America by a large group of Quakers headed by Herbert Hoover. For years afterwards we regarded all American visitors as our saviors, looking upon them in awe and fascination. To this day I find it difficult to leave food on my plate at the end of a meal.

The war had lasted four years; my father was away much of the time, at or near the Russian front, returning on leave only once or twice. I remember he had nightmares. I remember the old Emperor, Francis Joseph, taking a parade before the war. People were trained, from childhood, to adore him. There was a charming little legend about him – when he got to be very old he ate next to nothing; for lunch he only had a cup of chicken broth, which, however, was distilled from twenty-four chickens.

The only relief from the claustrophobia of the once brilliant city was escape into the huge, silent, snow-capped mountains, which I adored, and – above all – music. With my parents I heard many of this century's foremost artists in the Musikverein, Vienna's great concert hall. (Furtwängler, the king of conductors, patted me on the head when I asked him for an autograph; this was a most important event in my life.) My father, an excellent viola player, was often joined by friends for string quartet sessions in our apartment which lasted late into the evening; but none of this solved the question of my future profession.

It was, of course, considered absolutely necessary to have an academic degree and to be called 'Herr Doktor', no matter what one was a doctor of; in my case, the only practical answer seemed to be to study for a doctorate in law, which I duly tried and hated with a passion from the very first moment. In self-defense I spent as much time away from the university as I could get away with; instead of listening to boring lectures, I went to see the week's new movies (silent, of course), and was soon enthralled by King Vidor's *Big Parade*, von Stroheim's *Greed*, Dreyer's *Joan of Arc*, Eisenstein's *Potemkin*. A whole wide world of enchantment – a new art form full of unexplored possibilities – opened up before me. I began to see a life of adventure – elbow-room, open spaces, expeditions to unheard-of countries known only to Joseph Conrad. Dimly and excitedly I sensed that film, like music, offered a direct way to people's emotions: fascinating them, making them laugh or cry,

Seven years before the First World War the old Emperor was too frail to ride a horse, but he still liked parades, even when he had to stand.

8

My parents, 1907.

feel jubilant or angry. It could bypass reason and logic, depending on one thing alone: the movie-maker's imagination.

Together with a like-minded school friend I started hatching plans for a career in movies; it would be important to have a solid technical education if one was serious about it. Vienna was miles away from large film industries or schools. It turned out that there were then only two schools in all of Europe where one could study camera technique: one in Munich, the other in faraway Paris. We thought Paris would be great.

The next problem would be persuading my parents to go along with the shocking change I demanded in their expectation of my future. I had a strong feeling of security and a solid place within my family. I had enormous respect for my father, Dr Oskar Z., and I looked up to my mother, Anna – a charming, volatile person. There was also my baby brother, George, who would cry bitter tears whenever I played the violin, a marvelous grandmother and endless aunts, uncles and

cousins, all very involved in each others' problems, offering unrequested advice and, like most professional families, very conservative in their view of life.

The entire family was stunned when I broached my plan. The idea seemed grotesque, a calamity: I was throwing a promising, solid career to the winds. Theater people were glamorous, looked upon in awe mixed with suspicion, according to the Viennese motto 'Quick, put the silver away, the comedians are coming!' Film was, of course, infinitely worse, totally unserious and full of loose women. No wonder the entire family and particularly my poor mother were so upset – all their hopes dissolving because of my unrealistic pipe dreams.

All this was happening in 1927. Radio was in its infancy; no one had even imagined such a thing as television. Passenger planes flew short distances and were considered extremely hazardous. Normal people traveled by streetcar, railroad or steamer. There were horse-drawn coaches (*fiakers*) and even taxis but only the ultra-rich owned motor cars.

The Musikverein in Vienna.

After the first shock had passed, there was a strong reaction and much argument in the family, and then early one morning my father came in and sat quietly by my bed. We had a long talk and I tried to explain myself as best I could. Finally, he agreed to let me try the Paris school. I felt that he trusted me and knew I was serious. My mother hoped to the last that I would come to my senses sooner or later and return to a settled and sensible life.

So, off I went to Paris one lovely summer morning, leaving behind the city of my polite youth, giving up a loving family, music and mountains for many years to come; turning my back on the place where life seemed to be set in cement. People, having faced the twin horrors of unemployment and monstrous inflation, were now looking backwards to the vanished glory of Habsburg centuries; uneasy, bewildered, they were like so many canaries not daring to leave their cages even though the doors were now open.

In Austria, discrimination had been part of life since time immemorial. It was always there – oppressive, often snide, sometimes hostile, seldom violent. It was in the air and one sensed it at all levels, in school, at work and in society. A Jew was an outsider, a threat to the country's culture. Born in Austria, and raised as an Austrian, he would still never truly belong.

An Austrian brand of Fascism had now begun to flourish; the Nazis were but a cloud on the horizon but people no longer laughed at Hitler. His book, *Mein Kampf*, became obsessive reading, a gospel for millions. Boys came to school with swastikas in their lapels. 'Aren't you ashamed?' I asked one. 'I'm proud of it,' he said.

In 1927 no one could have imagined what was to come.

Left: *Comfort was not important at age nineteen.*

Right: *How I wish I could have been there.* (Photo: Dölf Reist)

Excited, but tired after twenty-six hours on the Paris train, I was met at the Gare de l'Est by my school friend Gunther von Fritsch, by now a six months' veteran at the brand new Technical School of Cinema, which was to give us both a solid background in our future profession. The principal, Professor Clerc, a world authority on photochemistry, was an imposing man with a huge beard full of ashes dropping from the Caporal cigarettes which hung limply from his lips. We studied photo-chemistry, optics and all sorts of other theory, all in French, and eventually graduated to operating the old hand-cranked Pathé movie camera, as well as the latest Debrie Parvo K. (The era of sound movies had not yet dawned in Europe.) We hand-developed the film negative on racks by time and temperature, learnt about density, gamma and contrast, and about printing and projecting the film we shot. After eighteen months of this we were well prepared to start work as assistant cameramen.

The more personal experience a director has had with the four main elements of film making – writing, acting, camera and editing – the more fully can he explore and extend the outer limits of their possibilities. For me, the camera, visual imagination and knowledge of what a lens can do were the starting point.

Almost from the instant of my arrival I felt free; the glass wall had disappeared, the sense of isolation was gone. Miraculously, people seemed to communicate openly and directly with each other.

Fritsch and I lived in a small pension next to the Luxembourg park, within walking distance of the school. Our lodging was fairly primitive: we had to use the public baths down the street; but Paris at age twenty was upbeat and wonderfully romantic. My father was sending me five hundred francs on the first day of each month, and for the first ten days one had a rather grand life. Afterwards it was coffee, bread and bananas for the rest of the month.

Montparnasse was then a joyful place, the Café du Dôme, the Rotonde and the 'Jockey' were the centre of things. People laughed, sang a lot, and danced in the streets on 14 July; Fujita and van Dongen were the great painters, I saw Fitzgerald and Hemingway from a distance and there was a fascinating experimental film group, the 'Avant-Garde' – René Clair, Cavalcanti, Man Ray, Germaine Dulac, Epstein and others. Their work

was shown in several specialized art-cinemas, the Vieux Colombier, Studio 28 and Studio Ursulines. Chevalier, Josephine Baker, Kiki and the Dolly Sisters reigned supreme. All this came to an end after eighteen months, as my French visa expired and I had to seek my fortune elsewhere. It was a great blow.

The next best place for film-makers then was Berlin, throbbing with energy, if not with romance and euphoria. Great German films were still being made by Pabst, Fritz Lang and others, even though Lubitsch and Murnau were already in Hollywood. Many Austrian and Hungarian writers, actors and directors had left stagnant Vienna and were active and successful in Berlin. It was, of course, a far cry from Paris but at least I had permission to work there and I assisted three different cameramen on as many films. The job involved loading and unloading film magazines, keeping lenses spotless, carrying the camera and tripod to where the chief wanted it and keeping the image in sharp focus. It kept me on the run, non-stop, and was, of course, excellent training. Working for a small, nervous company on a day when they had heavy expenses for three hundred extras, a catastrophe took place – and I was to blame. 'My' camera had run out of film in the middle of a scene! Everything came to a dead halt; people looked daggers at me. Clocks ticked unnaturally loudly; every second cost a fortune. All three hundred extras cooled their heels while I tore to the dark loading room I shared with Bob, another assistant, only to find that the door was locked from the inside. Unhappily, Bob was there with a girl. I do not remember walking back to the set or being fired but I know that I was skiing in Oberstdorf the next day. Having recovered from the shock I landed a job on another small film called *I Kiss Your Little Hand, Madame*, starring the popular Harry Liedtke and an earthy new girl called Marlene Dietrich, who was full of jokes and well-liked by the crew.

Finally, I was able to assist Eugen Schüfftan, a great cameraman who was working on a tiny film about two

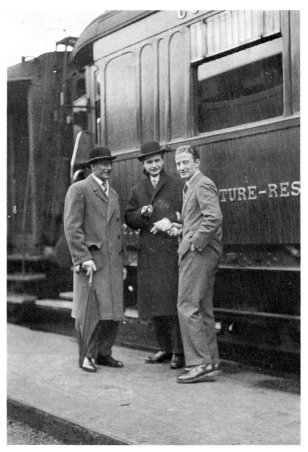

Top: *My father and my baby brother George, 1931.*
Bottom: *Friends seeing me off to Paris, 1927.*
Opposite: *Paris, 1925.* (Photo: André Kertész)

girls and their boyfriends spending a weekend on the Wannsee, a lake close to Berlin. The actors were amateurs, the director was the young Robert Siodmak, the writer a highly-strung young man named Billy Wilder. Edgar Ulmer also worked on the film, which was being made practically without any money at all. The sum total of my contribution was to carry the camera around and to stay out of trouble. It was out of the question to travel by automobile; we went to the location by bus and in the evening Billy and Siodmak took the exposed negative to the laboratory to be developed. One day they got into an argument and walked angrily off the bus, leaving the negative behind them – three days' work which was never seen again and had to be re-shot. The film was called *People on Sunday*, and its success surpassed everyone's wildest expectations. It became a cult film for many years afterwards and was hailed as a forerunner of neo-realism. But by then I was already in America.

In 1928 'talkies' had arrived in Europe. *The Jazz Singer* and *The Singing Fool* played to packed houses and the era of the silent film was, most regrettably, coming to a close: it was the end of movies as a universal, worldwide language. No one knew what the future would bring. Would there be room for the imagination and subtlety of the great directors – King Vidor, Lubitsch, Pabst, Fritz Lang? What about Chaplin and Buster Keaton and dozens of others? What about the great studios, Ufa and Terra? Would they all collapse?

Production all over Europe was slowing to a standstill, and at this point it seemed a good, if hazardous, gamble to go to Hollywood, to learn as much as possible about talking pictures, returning with a bit of expert knowledge. My parents consented, although they knew that it might be many years before we could see each other again. I received an American visa and a ship's ticket, tourist class, to New York. It would take seven days just to get across the Atlantic; California seemed incredibly remote, at the end of the earth.

Berlin had been fascinating in many ways – a tense, brilliant and decadent city, with wonderful theater, film and music; a place deep in political crisis, with ostentation and luxury and desperate unemployment side by side in a grotesque, surreal combination. As inflation and unemployment increased, the rich were moving further to the political right, the poor further to the left. German Conservatives became Nazis, Socialists became Communists. Emotion had long since begun to displace reason.

In the autumn of 1929 I sailed from Cherbourg aboard the *Leviathan*, a huge tub, originally called *Vaterland*, which had been ceded by Germany to the US as part of war reparations. It was a rough passage but there were many young people in tourist class and much laughter, fun and noise. Just once we were allowed to visit the

My school mate Gunther von Fritsch, who later became an excellent documentary film-maker.

At school in Paris, learning to hand-crank a silent movie camera (Debrie Model K). Two turns made sixteen frames per second.

first class, an enormous, sad mausoleum, silent except for the thud of the ship's engines, with immobile, very old, overdressed people sitting there like so many disconsolate dummies in a waxworks. To this day I remember a ghastly episode the morning after the storm-tossed first night aboard, stumbling groggily into the women's bathrooms, full of sick ladies. I can still hear their screams.

Arriving in New York at the end of October 1929, on 'Black Thursday', the fateful day of the huge Wall Street crash and the start of the Great Depression, we heard of ruined stockbrokers jumping out of skyscraper windows. We saw none of this from where the *Leviathan* was docking. In retrospect, this was perhaps not the best moment to arrive in America.

New York was a terrific experience, full of excitement, with a vitality and pace then totally lacking in Europe. It was as though I had just left a continent of zombies and entered a place humming with incredible energy and power.

The gates of adventure were opening. I still had five hundred dollars my father had given me in parting; it was then a serious amount of money and must have been a great sacrifice for my parents. I was not going to ask for more, ever. My English was reasonably good and I got along well except that I didn't know how to pronounce words I had not heard before. This led to odd scenes, such as asking for 'apple pee' at a drug store counter.

Two weeks in New York convinced me that hardly any 'real' movies were made there; Hollywood, a totally separate world, four days away by the fastest trains, seemed to be the only answer. Fritsch had preceded me to America and had a job in a commercial photographer's Manhattan studio; together we decided that I should go first and explore the situation. He would follow later. A plane trip was unheard of; trains were too expensive but a Greyhound bus would get me there in seven days.

The trip across America was a voyage of discovery.

Berlin, 1928. Harry Liedtke and a new girl, Marlene Dietrich. Unfortunately I was always busy loading film.

The bus was a primitive contraption, not stopping anywhere long enough for passengers to do more than two out of three essential things, so that one was either hungry, unshaven or bursting at the seams. But all this seemed unimportant; the impact of crossing the enormous continent was overwhelming. There was a sadness about the first part of the trip, forever passing ugly factories and smoke-filled skies, but once we crossed the Mississippi, it all changed and became marvelous.

The passengers were a mixed lot, curious about a foreigner and completely informal, seeming to accept me without suspicion. There was a warmth about them and a great deal of good-humored jokes and banter. Never mind who or what I was, or where I came from. They seemed trusting and, in a most touching way, quite innocent and vulnerable. At my age of twenty-two, I felt older than the forty-year-olds among them. I was jubilant in the certainty that this was the place where one could 'breathe free' and belong.

Once across North Platte, Nebraska, the highways became narrow and endlessly straight, two lanes constantly pointing West. Huge skies, lots of elbow room and the most spectacular sunsets. We followed the old Santa Fé trail, driving on through New Mexico, through Arizona, the old classic Wild West country, crossed the Colorado river and the Mojave desert and went on down, past miles of orange groves, into the bright lights of Los Angeles.

Apart from movies, oil and oranges, there was then no industry to speak of in southern California; few factories and no smog at all. On some evenings the scent of orange blossoms was in the air. No one ever locked the doors when leaving home for the day; people smiled at strangers and made corny jokes. There were no supermarkets, no super-highways, no super anything. Higher education was suspect. For girls, marriage was of supreme importance. You were supposed to go to college to be on the football team or to find the 'right' husband. To be a serious student or to like classical music was considered effeminate and not in tune with the rugged individualism of the times.

Family life was close-knit. Once a week the whole clan would wander to the movie theater to see the new program. For thirty-five cents per seat you could see a newsreel, a cartoon, a short subject, a B-picture and the A-picture, all carefully sanitized by the Hays Office. Almost all movies had the mandatory happy ending, with marriage the guarantee of eternal bliss. There was an orchestra or a Wurlitzer organ in the pit of the bigger theaters, but no popcorn as yet. Next to the trademark of the studio ('. . . if it's a Paramount Picture it's the best show in town' or 'Ars gratia Artis'), the movie stars were the most important thing in this microcosm; stories served as vehicles for them.

This huge tub took six days to cross the Atlantic, 1929.

Money had not yet achieved the status of a new religion.

Someone had told me about the Village Inn, a small hotel in the heart of Hollywood, next to the old Warner Brothers studio on Sunset Boulevard. (There is now a super-highway where it once stood.) For many months Fritsch and I lived there in the company of small-time actors who were usually out of work ('between pictures') and some interesting con-men; one drove a fancy Stutz-Bearcat car which had not been paid for. The one solid character in that insecure community was Leo White, a shriveled, elderly Cockney, who had played 'the Count' – an important character in Chaplin's early films.

It was my ambition to become a member of the cameramen's local union; my sponsor was none other than the famous Billy Bitzer, who had photographed most of D. W. Griffith's pictures. The union asked me for a two-hundred-dollar deposit. 'We'll let you know later,' they said. The answer arrived after six months. It was 'NO'. The money was duly returned, and that was the end of my camera career. I would probably still be an elderly focus puller if they had accepted me. Meanwhile, other things were happening: Gunther Fritsch landed a job as a labourer on the 'swing-gang' at RKO, where one of his duties was to help sweep the stages at the end of the day's shooting, and I fortunately had an introduction to Carl Laemmle, 'Uncle Carl', the head of Universal Studios, the makers of what were then known as 'tits-and-sand' pictures. He was a tiny old gentleman, very twinkly and friendly but clearly without the faintest idea of what to do with me. He ended the non-interview by pressing a button and passing me on to a casting director who asked, 'Have you been in the Army?' (meaning World War One of course; the next one was still in the pipeline, ten years away). I said no, I wasn't *that* old. He said, 'Well, never mind, you'll be a German soldier.' So they made me a German soldier and I was in *All Quiet on the Western Front* until I got fired. For a few days I was also a French ambulance driver.

Lewis Milestone, one of the great neglected Holly-

Wall Street, New York.

wood directors, was in charge. His dialogue director was the young George Cukor, who had just come West from the New York theaters. All the extras, including myself, were treated more or less like cattle. Normally, they got their jobs through the central casting office where they were registered. The motto of that office was 'Don't call us, we'll call you.' I remember extras dialing non-stop for hours trying to line up a job. This was before they were organized; things are different today.

'Our' extras were a mixed lot, many derelicts and drifters, people who couldn't hold down a job and some truly weird characters among them, but in addition to this flotsam and jetsam there were people of distinction

Above: *Approaching the Promised Land.* (Photo: Willard van Dyke)

Left: *Coming closer; Laguna, New Mexico, 1929.*

Top: *A real Western town, not a movie set – Oatman, Arizona, 1929.*

Middle: *Finally, Hollywood – the old Warner Brothers studio, Sunset Boulevard, 1929.*

Bottom: *Fritsch with his first car, a model-T Ford he bought for thirty-five dollars, 1930.*

who had fallen on hard times but had retained their style, along with a wardrobe, left from better days. There was a colorful but steadily diminishing colony of White Russian refugees in Hollywood in the 1920s, many of them aristocrats and high-ranking ex-officers who had fled from the Bolsheviks via Siberia and made a living, working as 'dress extras'. They could be trusted to look well in uniform or white tie and tails and to behave with confidence in any scene. I remember General Ikonikoff, a very dignified man, whose friends made a collection when he died broke. They bought the correct Russian military uniform from the Western Costume Company, together with exactly the right medals, and buried him, properly dressed for the occasion.

There were many attractive girls among these people; on the other hand, there was one middle-aged gent, a fellow Austrian, who tried to persuade me to have an affair with a call girl. He was prepared to pay, but wanted to watch. It was fascinating to be in the midst of all these goings-on; a chance to witness, from the worm's viewpoint, the thousand facets of uninhibited human behavior.

All Quiet on the Western Front was an enormous film with sets built on many different locations, partly on the back lot of Universal Studios and partly in Sherwood Forest, twenty miles from Hollywood, where we were taken by bus in the pre dawn December darkness. The shooting day started at 9.00 a.m; we did not get back to Hollywood until 8.00 p.m. – sometimes later. The production people kept us working hard and got their money's worth. Marching through deep mud in heavy artificial rain and wearing wet clothes all day was not necessarily a lot of fun; but sometimes there were days when we lounged on hospital cots, being bandaged.

Mr Milestone had very little time for talks with the six hundred extras; they were in the care of his first assistant, who, in turn, had a number of second and third assistants, sub-dividing the crowd into segments.

Top left: *Pretending to be a German soldier in* All Quiet on the Western Front, *1930. I'm the one in the white shirt.*
Bottom left: All Quiet *director Lewis Milestone and his dialogue director George Cukor, 1930.*

My first boss: director Berthold Viertel, 1930.

One experienced extra in each segment supervised the men of his own squad.

At the end of the sixth week I got into a dispute with the rude first assistant, who was drunk with power. I was promptly fired and thus ended my acting career. Having been paid seven dollars and fifty cents per day, I now had enough money to last for at least a month.

Soon afterwards, and by an enormous stroke of luck, I met Berthold Viertel, the distinguished Austrian stage and film director, recently imported from Berlin by Fox Studios. He needed a personal assistant. Mr Viertel was in his late forties, an irritable, brilliant intellectual, subtle and sensitive, deeply European in his reactions and terrified of the studio executives who didn't quite know what to make of him. His English was poor and American efficiency was alien and alarming to him. The bosses, in turn, were frightened by him and found him unpredictable. I had the great fortune of working with him for two years on scripts, casting and visual

Top: *Greta Garbo and Mr Viertel; Malibu, 1930.*
Bottom: *With my second boss, Robert Flaherty; Berlin, 1931.*

construction of scenes, learning about actors and acting, and about life in general.

Mr Viertel had three small sons; his ex-actress wife, Salka, one of the world's most generous and opinionated women, was famous in the European colony as a hostess and a champion purveyor of scintillating gossip. The people who came to the Sunday afternoon coffee-klatsches* at the Santa Monica house rendered me speechless and paralyzed by their presence: Eisenstein, who with his cameraman Tissé and the writer Alex-androv soon departed for Mexico, Murnau, Jacques Feyder, Dieterle, Max Reinhardt, sometimes Chaplin. Garbo, a great friend of Salka's, usually came all by herself, when the coast was clear. She was friendly and charming and terrified by her own mythical fame. Later, Salka wrote *Queen Christina* and a number of other screenplays for her.

The second son, Peter, grew into an enormously gifted and charming young writer and became a life-long friend; a firm believer in Pushkin's commandment 'You can't sleep with all the women in the world but you *must* try', and after a distinguished career as a *mujeriero* (lady-killer), he was lucky enough to meet and marry the wonderful Deborah Kerr.

Once or twice Robert Flaherty was among the guests, and this turned out to be 'destiny knocking at the door'. Having just come from Tahiti and the filming of *Tabu*, he was full of excitement over a new project, a movie about a remote tribe in Soviet Central Asia, and pre-paring to travel to Berlin for meetings with the Russians. I was still green and impressionable and very much in search of a hero; disenchantment with Hollywood and its castrated talents had begun to creep in.

(Fritsch had at the last possible moment talked me out of marrying a girl I didn't really like.) I was footloose; working on great documentary expeditions had always been my fondest dream. ('Documentary' was a baffling

* Gossip sessions attended by at least three people, usually female.

term in Hollywood in the 1920s. Harry Cohn, Columbia Studio's boss, defined it: 'It's a picture without women; if there is one woman in it then it's a semi-documentary.') Here was the 'father of the documentary', the man who had made *Nanook* and *Moana*, looking like some people's idea of God – silver hair atop an enormous head, pale blue eyes that could sparkle with sarcasm or blaze with indignation – truly an 'Irish poet with a camera'. There was an aura about him of freedom from convention, of endless horizons and the promise of a cleaner world somewhere just around the corner. Young people adored him. I still remember the story he told me about an American sailor on shore leave in Bombay in the 1920s; a Hindu priest guiding him through a temple showed him, with infinite reverence, an altar lamp which had been kept burning without interruption for many centuries; whereupon the merry sailor spat on his thumb and forefinger and, squeezing the wick, said, 'Well, it's out now!'

Invited to Hollywood, Flaherty entered the soft, glittering, neurotic community like a being from outer space. His ideas about film making were wildly premature and could not be absorbed into the dream manufacturing process. He didn't know the meaning of compromise and this quality attracted me to him above everything else.

So, I mustered the courage to ask him if I could be his assistant. He said 'Yes', if I could get to Berlin under my own steam. A few weeks later I returned to Europe aboard a small freighter via the Panama Canal. The next few months, sitting in Berlin waiting for Bob's future associates to agree to his ideas, were probably the most formative times of my life. We did very little work except for the testing of a few Newman-Sinclair cameras and some lenses. The true education came from drinking beer with Bob in the bar of the Adlon hotel, while listening to his long, rambling monologues and absorbing, by osmosis, his outlook on life and on picture making. In the end, nothing came of the venture and we both ran out of money. Bob went to England and made *Man of Aran* and I returned to America aboard the *Milwaukee*, after seeing my family in Vienna for the last time. His documentary approach was vivid in my memory when I prepared *The Search*, *The Men*,

Gregg Toland and his wife Helen, 1932. I wonder what he was telling her.

Buzz Berkeley. There were other activities besides looking for camera angles.

Radio City, New York, 1932. Building the future home of the 'Rainbow Room' on top of the tower.

High Noon, The Nun's Story, Julia and other movies. Professionally, he was my godfather.

In one of his more malicious moments, Bob was supposedly heard to say later on that I was the worst assistant he had ever had. I do hope he was kidding.

The Depression had started in earnest by that time, but no sooner had I disembarked in New York on a steamy, thunderous day in August 1931 than I had a job. Mr Viertel, who was in town preparing to direct a picture for Paramount, asked me to join him. He lived on the nineteenth floor of the St Moritz Hotel, and I had a room in a brownstone house on 54th Street. All night

the taxis crossing 6th Avenue would slam into second gear just below my window.

Shooting was to start daily at 9.00 a.m. at the Astoria Studios on Long Island – a good half-hour's drive from Mr Viertel's hotel, not counting traffic jams. At about 8.15 each morning I would find him, still in his dressing gown, happily ensconced in his room, having a leisurely breakfast and reading *The Times*, oblivious of the ticking of the clock.

There was sudden panic when he saw me, realizing that we might be late. This was followed by an agonizing hunt for his eyeglasses, his personal enemy, usually hiding underneath a mass of papers. Finally, we were off. Each morning, just as the door clicked shut, he would realize that he had forgotten something – but had left the key *inside*. I laughed at his antics, unaware that I would be waging the same battles fifty years later.

The title of the film was *The Wiser Sex*, with an excellent cast ... Claudette Colbert, Melvyn Douglas, Lillian Tashman, Franchot Tone and Irving Pichel. Several people became life-long friends: George Folsey and his camera operator, Joe Ruttenberg (a few years later both were top cameramen at MGM), and Frank Cavett, the brilliant first assistant, a moody red-headed Welshman.

On Sundays I liked to take photos in the empty downtown streets of New York. There was a savage beauty about the place when not a soul was in sight. I can't remember much about the film except that I disliked the rushes and wished I could quit. It was with a sigh of relief I greeted the news that my appendix was in bad shape and had to come out immediately. Shooting finished while I was in hospital and I was free to return to Los Angeles, which I did in February, by steamship via the Panama Canal.

Gunther Fritsch met me in San Diego and we had a memorable drive across the lovely, blossoming spring landscape of California.

1932 turned out to be a very good year, by and large. Fritsch and I moved into a house in Santa Monica Canyon. We knew lots of young hopefuls, among them David Flaherty, Bob's younger brother, a gentle, sensitive Irishman. Bob had given me a letter of introduction to Arthur Hornblow, one of Sam Goldwyn's executives, later a very good friend, who took me to meet the great man and to see of what use, if any, I could be to the company. 'What do you think of American pictures?' Goldwyn asked me. 'They are too slick,' I said. Goldwyn looked helpless; Hornblow quickly got me out of the room and invented a spectacular, if not rational, job for me: Busby Berkeley was then rehearsing dance numbers for an Eddie Cantor musical, *The Kid from Spain*, with Gregg Toland as cameraman. *My* duty was to suggest unusual and exciting camera angles to *them*(!). (This was, of course, long before Buzz became the great Mr Berkeley and long before Gregg's work on *Citizen Kane*.)

The Eddie Cantor musicals were a yearly event,

preceded by a vast, month-long search for the most beautiful girls in America. Close to a thousand candidates across the nation were interviewed by talent scouts; the chosen fifty, now called 'Goldwyn Girls', would appear in Hollywood – wide-eyed, totally dazzled by all the glamor and quite unaware of studio hierarchy. For two weeks the crew had a great time with them; once the girls understood who was what, they disappeared in the executive-directorial stratosphere.

Among our Hollywood friends was a young writer, Bill Drake, a charming, most generous man. Upon seeing my New York photos he thought I should go back there and try doing a book of photographs of the town. He encouraged many young people and handed out money right and left. Apparently I was the only person who ever paid him back.

David Flaherty came along as a passenger in my small Model-A Ford Roadster, paying for gas on the cross-country trip to New York. The speakeasy culture was still going strong in spite of legal Prohibition, but it was clear that the Depression had bitten very deep. There was no Social Security then; men in their sixties were selling apples in the street; there were soup kitchens in Times Square. I had permission to climb to the top of Radio City, which was still being built, and to take pictures from what is the 'Rainbow Room' now and was an airy scaffolding then. I spent the winter in the city taking pictures, still living on 54th Street, skimpily eating at a cafeteria around the corner. In November Roosevelt was elected President; a huge crowd filled Times Square, reading the latest reports on the flickering Times Building board. I had the good luck to capture the unique moment of his landslide victory; he had carried all states except Maine and Vermont. The next day someone put up a sign on the Vermont border, reading 'You are now leaving the United States'.

I met a number of David's friends, some of whom became my life-long friends also: Henwar Rodakiewicz, a Harvard-educated Polish-American, a great, generous documentary director who owned a Rolls-Royce and little else, and the brilliant photographer Floyd Crosby and Aliph, his wife.

When it became clear that no one would be buying a book of photographs at the price of five dollars in those

Wall Street, New York, 1932, during the Depression. A sign of the times.

Are Here Again', were symbols of the new mood.

The trip through Georgia, New Orleans, Texas and New Mexico was complicated by the President's order to close down all banks in the country for a while. Checks could not be cashed; the only way to get enough gas for my Ford was to take aboard hitch-hikers who, desperate for jobs, were trying to get from one place to another where the grass might be greener and who would gladly pay a few cents for transportation.

Crowd in Times Square, waiting to hear the result of the Presidential elections, November 1932.

perilous times, Frank Cavett most generously loaned me twenty dollars, as my money had run out and I had to drive back to California. (I found out later that this was all the money he had in the bank at the time.) The photographic venture thus coming to an inglorious end, I started on the long voyage home. It was March and Roosevelt was being inaugurated as President. Somewhere in South Carolina I heard his acceptance speech on the radio: 'Americans have nothing to fear but fear itself.' The effect was electric; an era of optimism was on its way. Disney's song 'Who's Afraid of the Big Bad Wolf?' and Roosevelt's campaign song, 'Happy Days

The precise moment of Roosevelt's victory. His picture has just appeared on the screen, top left.

Hitchhiking was not the lethal hazard it is today; people were kind and helpful during the Depression, as everyone was in the same boat.

I made it back to Hollywood and joined Fritsch – who had meanwhile become Basil Wrangell's assistant cutter at MGM – living in a charming, ramshackle old apartment house on Honey Drive in Laurel Canyon. Mr Viertel was fortunately about to start another film at Paramount, *The Man from Yesterday*, with Charles Boyer, Claudette Colbert and Clive Brook. I was happy to be invited aboard and to meet Oliver Garrett, the writer who became one of my heroes, and the very tough first assistant director, Henry Hathaway, another great friend in later years. Ray June and Karl Struss were the cameramen and a fine time was had by all.

Later in the year there was a research job at Goldwyn's. The company had signed a Russian actress, Anna Sten, in vain hopes of making her a great star. She played the lead in *Nana*, with Dorothy Arzner directing. Gregg Toland did a lovely job of photography, unfortunately to no avail. An ominous quiet settled down once that assignment was finished.

The Wave
(1934)

Toward the end of 1933 – still in the depths of the Great Depression – there was word from Mexico. My friend Henwar, who was there preparing to direct a full-length documentary for the newly progressive Government, found that he had to leave the job because of an earlier commitment. Would I be interested in taking over? The picture was to be made for the Federal Department of Fine Arts, headed by the composer Carlos Chavez. The producer would be Paul Strand, already a distinguished photographer, who would also be in charge of the camera work. As a civil service employee I would earn the princely sum of one hundred and forty pesos (about twenty-five dollars) per week, plus expenses for travel, food and housing. The shooting was to take four months.

It all sounded exotic and exciting. I accepted in indecent haste, boarded the narrow-gauge train from El Paso, Texas, for a slow, jolting, fascinating three-day trip to Mexico City and was met by Henwar and Paul Strand – a very serious man in his forties – and by two

The funeral procession.

enthusiastic young men who were to assist in my virgin effort as director, Agustín Velasquez Chavez and Emilio Gomez Muriel.

The film – the first (and last) of its kind – was expected to play a small part in the Government's plan to educate millions of illiterate citizens throughout the enormous country and bring them out of their isolation; for thousands of remote hamlets and villages the horizon was still the end of the world; people living in the tropics could hardly imagine a way of life in the cold, high plateau country – nor could miners have any idea of fishermen's lives. It was hoped that films might help to extend their awareness of each other as compatriots sharing the same human problems. 'Our' picture was to dramatize the lives of fishermen on the Gulf Coast.

Much preparatory work had already been done. A script of sorts existed and the leading man, an athletic, clean-cut university student, Silvio Hernandez, had been chosen by Henwar and Paul. Although not an actor, he did well, playing the fishermen's leader in fighting the boat-owners for the chance of a better life. The location was already set and fairly primitive equipment was assembled, including a silent Akeley camera (Strand's, I believe) normally used on expeditions. The entire film would have to be hand-cranked and there would be no sound – the dialogue was to be synchronized later. A

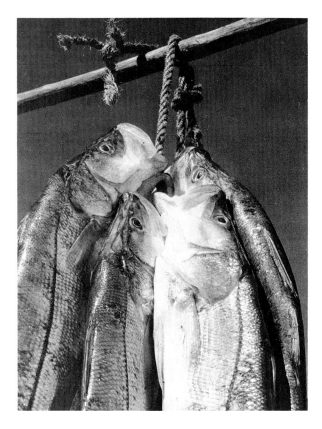

famous Mexican composer, Silvestre Revueltas, was to write the score.

Henwar departed and I was on my own. We soon left Mexico City – then still a friendly, unhurried colonial town, where the lively Arts were blossoming, thanks to brilliant writers, musicians and painters such as Diego Rivera, Orozco and Siqueiros – and descended first to Veracruz, then thirty miles south to the chosen location, the small fishing town of Alvarado, spread along the banks of an enormous lagoon, fed by the great river Papaloapan. Those last miles were the most colorful – there were no roads through the bush; the only means of transport was an ancient open streetcar powered by a four-cylinder Ford Motor, of which the natives said '*sale cuando quiere, llega cuando puede*'– 'it starts when it wants to and gets there when it can'. The passengers were mostly Indian peasants, carrying trussed chickens, live iguanas and the occasional armadillo. The bush had to be kept from blocking the track by weekly machete-wielding crews.

We were greeted by a pungent smell of fish even before Alvarado came in sight. The place was famous all over Mexico as '*el pueblo el màs malhablado en toda la republica*'– 'the most foul-mouthed village in the entire country'. The inhabitants of the region – the Jarochos – swore not just in four-letter words but in paragraphs, surpassing in imagination even the Hungarians and Russians. This was where I learnt to speak Spanish.

The town lived on fishing. Every few months, large schools of haddock would come down the river, heading out to sea, keeping the town humming for a week or two before it sank back into lethargy. Thanks to the amazing fertility of the land no one went hungry. The people were poor but that did not seem to interfere with their joy of life. Friendly, generous and of a very sudden temperament, they laughed and sang a lot, drank *aguardiente* and, when drunk enough, would become belligerent, yank out their machetes and, once in a great while, kill each other. On fiesta days a platform went up next to the plaza's bandstand and we learned to take a few turns dancing the *huapango* and *zapateado* or *la bamba* with them – dances mostly depicting the courtship of rooster and chicken.

Our house, beside the lagoon, was large, airy, whitewashed, with tiled floors and scrupulously clean; still, in dark corners one could see tarantulas moving slowly, crab-wise, like solitary hairy hands. Once a sudden bark next to my ear woke me up. Inside my mosquito net,

The fish buyer.

Above: *This is where we lived for ten months.*
Right: *Across the river, where the poor folks lived.*

sitting on the pillow, was a tiny, transparent lizard, looking at me with beady black eyes. There had been a fiesta the night before and lots of tequila to drink; now I thought I was having the DTs. But he was real enough and I flung him off, quickly. I learned that his kind was called *perrito* – 'little dog' – because of the bark, and that this was the only poisonous lizard in the region. We also got used to the sight of snakes – there were pythons upstream – and of occasional hammerhead sharks and manta rays.

The seven months of life in Alvarado turned out to be a magical experience. I wouldn't have missed it for anything in the world, although it had soon become crystal clear that the planned four-month shooting schedule was unrealistic; the work would take at least twice as long. The choice was simple: resign immediately and leave, or stay and take your chances in this very uncertain enterprise.

Time stood absolutely still in Alvarado. It had no reality and no importance whatsoever. When we started shooting, at 7.30, the heraldic-looking *zopilotes*

(buzzards) on the rooftops were still drying their spread wings in the morning sun; after 10.30 its near vertical rays could no longer reach the actors' faces beneath their wide-brimmed sombreros; besides, the heat had become ferocious. We stopped for a good four hours' siesta – a great invention; lying in one's hammock one could read, reflect on life or write letters. Then we would shoot again from three until close to sunset. It was a full life, in spite of the lack of frantic external activity. The evenings were quiet – if there wasn't a fiesta. The local movie theater stood empty; once in a while, a furtive man would show up with a load of 'blue' movies, and nine months later there would be a rash of new babies.

We had recruited practically all 'actors' from among the local fishermen, who needed to do no more than be themselves. They were splendid men and loyal friends, and working with them was a joy. Soon they began calling me 'Mr Fré'. In addition to acting, they carried all our equipment, rowed the boats and did a multitude of other jobs, earning more money than

Above left: *Young Felipe (age ten).*

Above right: *Old Felipe (age eighty).*

Left: *Tobias at work, hauling the net.*

Above: *The fish are not moving.*
Right: *Antonio Lara mending a net.*

Paul Strand hand-cranking his Akeley camera.

We even had a wooden camera platform.

ever before – forty-five cents per day, per man – and enjoying themselves hugely. Most of us lost the habit of money after a few weeks as it was pretty useless locally; there was hardly anything you could buy with it except perhaps the skin of a python or alligator from the old German trader. Our salaries kept building up in the bank in Mexico City and, just as on a sailor's shore leave, we blew it all in one night when we finally got back. I say 'we' because meanwhile Henwar had returned and with him my friend Gunther von Fritsch, who did a heroic job editing the film – and Ned Scott,

There was a lot of free time for landscaping a beard.

whose photographs became classics. When I had sunstroke, Henwar, with Emilio's assistance, directed the dialogue scenes and one or two other important episodes.

Paul Strand and I did not get on too well. While nominally the boss, he was defensive about his lack of production experience; but much more important was the fact that he, as a stills photographer, saw films as a succession of splendid but motionless compositions, while I was trying my utmost to get as much movement into scenes as possible.

In all this time, only one small disaster occurred: black-bearded Felipe Rojas, a fisherman who played the foreman, decided right in the middle of a sequence we were shooting in July that the beard made him too hot. Next morning he appeared on the set, handsome and clean-shaven. We had to shoot 'around' him for two months before his beard was of any use to us.

The exposed negative was sent all the way back to Roy Davidge's laboratory in Los Angeles. It took four weeks before we could see our rushes, projected on the white walls of the living room. There was no electricity in town during the day and this paralyzed the moviola we needed for editing. Fortunately, Henwar had the idea of mounting it on a footpedal-operated Singer sewing machine, with a flashlight illuminating the frame. It was the only way and it worked – although I can't say that it speeded progress.

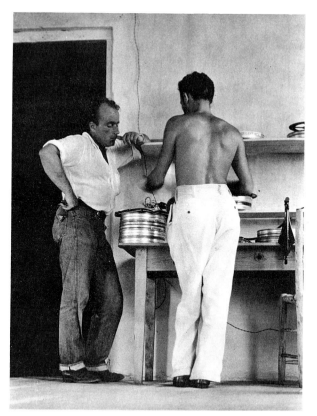

Henwar and I in the cutting room.

I should have worn a hat like everybody else. Soon afterwards I had a sunstroke.

The shooting was finished in October. The budget ran out at the same time and our salaries stopped; there was no way of knowing if they would ever be resumed. Clearly there was nothing else to do but return home – the East Coast for Paul, Henwar and Ned; Los Angeles for Gunther and me. The complete rough cut was delivered to the Government and technically very poor sound was added later under Emilio's supervision. Most of the cut survived without changes, but additions were made in New York afterwards, without my knowledge.

We flew back just in time for Christmas. In Los Angeles I was immediately struck by the general air of haste, of drivers madly racing their cars to beat a traffic light. 'Why the hurry?' I thought. Two days later I was doing the same.

On the top floor of MGM I saw top executives led by Mr Mayer emerging from a conference – sad millionaires, elderly, with paunches and limp cigars. I couldn't help thinking of the penniless, laughing and drunken Jarochos enjoying life to the hilt.

The film's original title, *Pescados* (a double meaning – 'fish' or 'trapped'), was later changed to *Redes* ('nets'). In English it was called *The Wave*. For a film of its kind it was quite successful, especially in France. I'm told that some years later the Nazis found the negative in Paris and burned it. A few prints still exist.

Apprentice and Journeyman
(1935–1942)

Camping in the High Sierra, 1940.

Below left: *Tim, age three, 1943.*
Below right: *Renée Bartlett, 1935.*

There is confusion in my mind about the year 1935. I remember a few important things:

Early in the year, Bob McIntyre, Sam Goldwyn's production manager and a good friend since *The Kid from Spain*, asked me to do research for a film to be directed by Sidney Franklin – a re-make of *The Dark Angel*, the romantic World War One love story originally played by Vilma Banky and Rod la Rocque. It was pleasant and interesting to be working with Mr Franklin, even from a distance.

In spring, Henry Hathaway, who had become an important director at Paramount after directing *Bengal Lancers*, asked me to be his personal assistant and to direct a few second units on *Peter Ibbetson*, starring Gary Cooper and Ann Harding; this is how I met Renée Bartlett, a tall, blonde, handsome English girl, a Viking type, who was working in the costume department. One word led to another; fifty years later we are still married. Nothing, especially not a studio romance, could have been kept secret from a film crew or from their freely

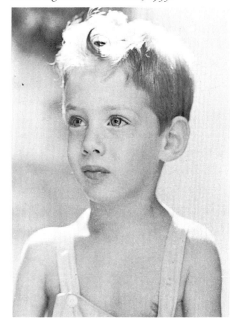

offered comments and advice. A splendid son, Tim, appeared five years later, just as the battle for Dunkirk was at its height. (As a four-year-old he asked us, 'Why is it OK when we bomb the Germans and why is it not OK when they bomb us?')

After *Peter Ibbetson*, jobs became very scarce indeed. Savings disappeared, but fortunately Renée kept on working at around twenty-five dollars a week and supported us both for almost a year. The rest of 1935 was barren, except for one memorable three-day stint in November, again organized by Bob McIntyre at Goldwyn's. There was a single scene, set in a Viennese coffee-house in William Wyler's *Dodsworth*; my job, as technical adviser, was to see that the costumes and the general atmosphere were correct and in period. Working on the set, it seemed to me that Mr Wyler, who was rehearsing the scene and lining up the camera, was overlooking a very effective angle. Full of innocence and stupid enthusiasm, I approached him, saying, 'Excuse me, don't you think that scene would look better from this other angle?' Mr Wyler looked at me in total disbelief; I could see that he was about to get angry. Suddenly, he laughed and said, 'You know, I did exactly the same thing when I was a messenger at Universal and had to go on sets. I offered my advice and the directors had me thrown off the set.' He, of course, did nothing of the sort. I admired that man enormously, always. At some point during that year, either on *Dodsworth* or on *Dark Angel*, I remember meeting the young writer Lillian Hellman.

1936 was a pretty grim year on the job front, but quite marvelous in every other way. With hindsight, it seems impossible to realize how little we knew about what was going on in the rest of the world, where the sky was darkening. Europe seemed incredibly remote, with letters taking more than two weeks to arrive and Hearst's *Examiner* being the fountainhead of news. Reading Louella Parsons' gossip column seemed more important than worrying about Mussolini or Ethiopia. Only the Spanish Civil War caused some excitement. At that time, only some fifty years ago, there was a worldwide outcry when, for the first time in history, an entire town and its population were wiped out by bombardment from the air. Those Americans who

Cameraman Karl Freund and Garbo in Camille *(MGM, 1936). Freund was the man who asked his assistant to come wash his car on a Sunday.*

supported the Spanish Republican side were likely to be accused of 'premature opposition to fascism' later on. It was like being on the moon.

With the help of Salka Viertel – and perhaps Garbo – there was a brief job in August, working with George Cukor, who was directing *Camille*. It was not his fault that it turned out to be a frustrating experience. Henwar and Ned had meanwhile moved to Hollywood and joined Gunther and me, each with his own apartment in Honey Drive. I'm not sure how we managed to make a living, but the fact of being jobless did not seem all that serious, even though it was irritating. As there was nothing better to do, Henwar and I wrote a Mexican story called *Bonanza*, which was later sold to MGM as a vehicle for Wallace Beery but was never made.

The Wave finally appeared for a brief run at the Filmarte Theater in Hollywood. A Goldwyn executive, Reeves Espy, one of the few people who saw it, talked about it to an acquaintance, Jack Chertok, the head of the MGM Shorts Department.

After many months, in February 1937, there was a most welcome job offer – research at MGM for *The Emperor's Candlesticks* – a mediocre story situated in Austria, with George Fitzmaurice directing. The head of the department was Nathalie Bucknall, a White Russian who had fought in the Women's Death Battalion against the Bolsheviks and had escaped via Siberia. The senior technical director was a charming ex-Austrian Imperial

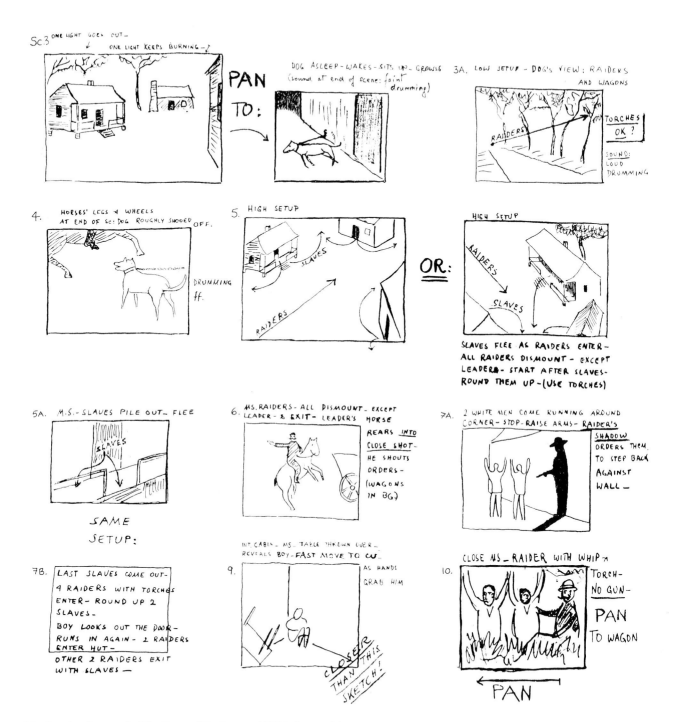

My thumbnail notes for The Story of Dr Carver, MGM *short subject, 1937.*

Cavalry captain, George Richelavie, who became a dear friend. At first, all went well, until suddenly a Russian sequence was written into the script. Knowing nothing about Russian uniforms, I made several mistakes and was fired. To my surprise, I found myself back again at MGM a few weeks later.

After two years of uncertain fortunes (1935–6) the break had finally come: Jack Chertok, who had seen excerpts from *The Wave*, asked me to direct a silent ten-minute movie for narration by Pete Smith. There was no contract and one could be fired at the end of any week. The salary was small but this allowed for an excellent working condition: *plenty of time to prepare a subject properly so that it could be shot without confusion or delays.*

As it turned out, I served my apprenticeship in that department for more than three years; next to Flaherty and *The Wave*, it became a most important learning experience. The place was a reservoir and testing ground for budding directors and writers – Jules Dassin, George Sidney and Jacques Tourneur were among the tadpoles. This was in line with the fiercely competitive policy of all the studios: to own the biggest possible stable of *talent*, the irreplaceable lifeblood of the industry, with actors, writers and directors tied down and immobilized by long-term contracts. Scouts were searching everywhere: the New York stage, the opera, schools and drug stores and, of course, European films and theaters (Garbo, Dietrich, Lubitsch). Sometimes people would be hired at enormous salaries and then kept on ice without assignment, simply to foil the competition. I recall Scott Fitzgerald wandering aimlessly around the MGM lot and the legend of Dorothy Parker who, after months of lonely frustration, had a painter put the word 'MEN' on her office door.

With rare exceptions, directors tended to be middle-aged (thirty-five!) or older in the 1930s; it took a long time to work up through the ranks and to gain the basic experience. MGM was perhaps the only company to bring in, from nowhere, young people suspected of having talent (there were of course a few relatives mixed in) and to groom them tentatively to see what would happen. This was largely due to the shrewdness and

intelligence of Chertok and his young assistant, Dick Goldstone, who established a list of interesting projects. I was fortunate to be assigned to a series on great physicians – Semmelweis, Bruce, Goldberger, Banting/Best – and later to the ambitious *Crime Does Not Pay* series, shot with real on-stage dialogue and taken seriously by audiences firmly believing, only forty years ago, in the majesty and authority of the law. Today, such a title would be greeted with unbounded hilarity.

There were three important disciplines built into the work, which forced us to develop our imagination:

The *story* had to be told in ten and a half minutes (one reel equals one thousand feet of film). In one case I was coping with the entire life story – from babyhood to age ninety – of the great black scientist Dr Washington Carver. You could not help learning about concise storytelling.

The *budget* was fixed and exceedingly small; one-third of it we never saw, as it was a charge for 'overhead'

The start of my career: directing dogs, 1937.

(studio maintenance), including such things as the MGM restaurant. This meant extreme economy in building sets, casting and numbers of extras. (We once needed a crowd of onlookers to watch a large fire in a city hospital, at night. For the crowd we were given *ten* people! We dressed one as a policeman who, facing us, pushed the triangular multitude towards us, their backs to the camera. If that 'mob' had moved three inches sideways you would have seen thin air next to them.)

The *shooting schedule* was fixed at four days per reel and, as it was impossible to work in sequence, we shot wildly out of continuity, sometimes starting at the last scene in the script. Moving shots were frowned upon, as it took too long to set them up. Crane shots were, of course, only a wish-dream. You had to be very sure about the place each single set-up had in the overall story. (I made primitive sketches of key shots, but disliked formal storyboards. To me, they are like a contract, making things rigid and freezing the all-important flow of free improvisation.)

There were a number of pitfalls: crew members were trained by their departments – camera, sound, make-up, hair, costume – to achieve technical perfection. The

Pier Angeli before and after glamorization at MGM. Young actors sometimes did not recognize themselves after they had been done over. They didn't know who they were; they never had a chance to find out. All this changed after the era of long contracts came to an end.

stars had to look flawless, every hair in place, even if they had just emerged from a hurricane. The director was sometimes asked to repeat a perfectly good scene because of some small technical fault, and the sad result would finally emerge polished but stale and quite dead. The slates of quite a few classic shots bear a chalked comment by cameramen wishing to protect their jobs: 'SHOT UNDER PROTEST'. I quickly learned to discourage most of these antics and to insist on energy and spontaneity.

All of this proved to be invaluable training when the time came for shooting complicated, jigsaw-puzzle pictures like *High Noon*, in twenty-eight days, or *From Here to Eternity*, in forty-one.

To this day, I prefer the earliest takes; I sometimes even shoot rehearsals, when unexpected stumbles and small accidents happen. This is, of course, a purely personal matter. The illustrious Willie Wyler was known to shoot endless takes before he had what he wanted. George Stevens used to cover a scene from all possible angles and end up with huge masses of film to choose from. John Ford not only shot very few takes but used to camera-cut, shooting sometimes only one single line of dialogue in a given set-up, in order to prevent the studio from re-cutting the film. 'If they haven't got it, they can't use it,' he said. No 'protection' shots for him. The same goes for Billy Wilder.

Many actors, especially non-professionals, are at their best in early takes; they lose energy and flatten out as they go on repeating themselves over and over. Others, like Montgomery Clift, use each take as a rehearsal, a chance to add new detail, enriching the scene as they go on. Still others can't remember their lines until the fourth or fifth take.

In the early 1940s a decline in the status of directors had set in, brought about by the advent of 'talkies' and a mass-production mentality gaining ground in studio management. Directors were downgraded and treated like foremen running assembly lines. Finally, a small, prominent group decided the time had come to establish an organization, to be called the Screen Directors' Guild, in order to defend their members and the quality of their work against the spread of factory methods.

The studios reacted with immediate suspicion. At

King Vidor

George Stevens

William Wyler

It has been my good fortune to have known these seven men. Most of them were my friends and teachers. To this day I am in awe of them.

John Ford

Billy Wilder

David Lean

John Huston

MGM all shorts directors were called – one by one – to the front office and advised, in a fatherly way, that joining the Guild could present career problems in the future. Almost all of us joined within the next few days.

For us, those early days at the Guild were pure euphoria. Imagine the thrill of sitting at a table next to one's heroes, being treated as a colleague by the likes of John Ford and George Stevens and listening to them talk about movies! It was a kind of mutual-admiration society, *strongly devoted to the pursuit of excellence*, and it grew into a strong industrial organization, renaming itself the Directors' Guild of America.

In 1941 Jack Chertok, promoted to the post of B-picture producer, asked me to direct his first movie, *Kid Glove Killer*, with Van Heflin, Marsha Hunt and Lee Bowman. Mindful of the austerity of the Shorts Department I decided, at the first production meeting, to ask for a crane. There were no raised eyebrows, only the question 'Do you want the medium or the big one?' This was the moment when I knew I had arrived: no longer an apprentice, I had become a journeyman.

I was now under contract. Before being given a full-length picture to direct it was compulsory to sign up for seven years, with small raises and options every six months. I didn't quite grasp that these were standard one-way options: MGM could fire me but I couldn't quit, and anything I might write or any idea I might have would automatically become MGM property. Neither did I perceive that, in exchange for steady employment and enormous chances for more learning, the tiny print of legal clauses implied obedience to all instructions and acceptance of whatever script might be assigned to me; and while I would be consulted and could argue and insist on my opinions, the company had the final word on everything: script, dialogue, casting, editing. Studios insisted on covering the important key scenes of their films with 'protection shots'. While these were mostly boring and unnecessary long shots of the entire scene, they gave the studio its only chance to re-edit a picture upside down if they wanted to. The studios had that kind of power then: contracts allowed them to change actors' names, invent new personalities for them, cap their teeth, change the color of their hair and interfere with their private lives.

For film people there was hardly a place other than Hollywood to go to. Stars, directors and writers could be loaned out to other companies at a price greater than their salaries, the 'parent' studio keeping the difference for itself.

Shorts subjects directors without current assignment were nevertheless kept on the payroll, but were expected to direct second units (without principal actors) and casting tests of hopeful actor-candidates. In this way I shot tests that led to contracts for the young Elizabeth Taylor, Esther Williams and Keenan Wynn, and I 'directed' a chimp in a scene for *Tarzan*, after explaining to the producer that the scene was stupid and totally unnecessary. He disagreed, seemed irritated and said that the studio insisted on my shooting it. I didn't know it then, but it soon became clear that I was not meant to be a company man.

Each of the studios was bound to reflect the personality of the man at the top. Paramount was an enormously friendly place, almost like a family and full of pleasant, earthy gossip. Most people liked each other, knew all the intimate details of each others' lives and laughed a lot (I found this out when I met and courted Renée Bartlett, who was working there). MGM was earnest and sanctimonious; there was an aura of people being wary and suspicious. At Columbia the air was charged with fear, because of the tyrannical ways of Harry Cohn, the studio chief. But it was a good studio for directors – Frank Capra started there, Leo McCarey, Stevens, Boleslavsky. Jack Warner ran his studio with an iron hand; he even barred his own son from entering. United Artists (Goldwyn, Pickford, Fairbanks) was perhaps the most pleasant place of all. Nice people worked there.

In the 1930s many pictures were full of cloying sentimentality. Production went forward on factory principles and under controlled industrial conditions, assuring a steady flow of 'product' from the assembly line. The average director was supposed to function as a foreman, mixing the ingredients – sets, costumes,

L. B. Mayer (Studio Chief, MGM).   *Jack Warner (Chief, Warner Brothers).*   *Ed. Mannix (General Manager, MGM).*

actors, props, script – into the finished movie. Distant locations were unpopular, because hard to control; on stage, the weather – fog, rain, snow – could be manufactured, and there were vast back lots with permanent standing sets: Western streets, cathedrals, palaces. Censorship, administered by the Breen office, an over-reaction to earlier abuses, was strict and all-pervasive. The villain had to get his just punishment, always; in horizontal love scenes, on couch or bed, one of four feet had to firmly touch the floor. No wonder creative people – especially writers – were resentful and sarcastic about the way they had to work and the mush they had to concoct. But the tennis was pleasant, taxes were low and the sun shone day after day.

For learning, MGM was ideal. They considered themselves the greatest. Warners and Columbia went for realism, of sorts; MGM went for glamor.

The top man at MGM was Louis B. Mayer, probably the most powerful man in Hollywood, hated by many, liked by few, feared by most. It was he who collected the greatest stable of stars, superstars and starlets and who set the studio's style: 'There are only two kinds of women – mothers and whores,' he said, and 'Don't forget that the audience is twelve years old. Tell them everything three times: before it happens, when it's happening and after it has happened,' and 'The star's

face must always be seen, even if it's midnight in a tunnel.' Still it was he, more than anyone else in Hollywood, who invented Garbo and many other stars.

L. B. Mayer had an extraordinary instinct for what the audience wanted and, like all studio heads, he insisted on happy endings. And yet an issue of *Cahiers du Cinéma*, at that time the Bible of film buffs everywhere, claimed that the best pictures to come out of Hollywood were made in the 1930s, the time when the factory system was at its height.

A champion hypocrite, Mayer could cry real tears whenever it suited his plans. He loved power and used it to make men cringe and women comply. While I was still in the Shorts Department he decided that George Sidney, Dassin and I were 'his boys'. Dassin used to get nervous when Mr Mayer put his arm around his shoulder because 'his hand was too close to my throat'.

Mr Mayer had a lot of executives and department heads, some very fine and able, some less so. He considered producers the single most important element in picture making. Next came the star, then the story. In fourth place was the director. There were some excellent producers on the lot and – because of a remarkable amount of nepotism – quite a few others who, exuding an aura of anxiety and nervousness, were simply determined to hang on to their jobs, come what may. These latter – the original 'yes' men – were regarded with special disdain by the directors. When the studio became top-heavy with relatives there would be a house cleaning, usually every March. The opening shot was always the firing of one certain lady, L. B. Mayer's niece (who had a writer's job but did not write); everyone knew this to be a signal for the massacre that was to follow. After forty to fifty people had been disposed of, the niece was quietly put back on the payroll.

I believe that each year MGM had to deliver fifty-two pictures to its parent company, Loew's Inc., who were the sales department, always spoken of as 'the boys in New York', who distributed the 'product' in their own chain of theaters. As in most major film companies, they dictated the release dates, the advertising and schedules and tried to dictate how to make 'good' pictures. Forever unable to grasp that movies can't be manufactured like salami, they would send hapless efficiency experts to impose their logic on us; when studios tried to follow their suggestions the result was almost invariably a disaster. Fortunately, those mercantile souls were four days' travel away from Los Angeles and their visits were brief. Unhappily, having moved to Hollywood long ago, they now have a strong grip and control over the creative work.

There was A-'product' and B-'product', the latter made to fill the double-feature bills. B-pictures were shot very quickly, in a tense, apprehensive and disrespectful atmosphere, with indifferent stories and cynical crews. They were like a way station in people's careers, a platform where the paths of enthusiastic directors and actors on their way up to A-pictures crossed with those of their middle-aged, disgruntled colleagues descending from the Elysian fields of stardom. (Once, after an unhappy downgraded director had finished shooting a scene, I heard him say, 'Print it and f... it.')

I'm afraid I have made the place sound like a living hell. Far from it; it was in fact very pleasant. The long-term associations made for close ties, almost a family feeling, with genuinely nice people – colleagues, actors, writers, cameramen, grips, gaffers, prop-men. Most important, there was a continuity and steady development in one's work. Movie-makers had not yet been turned into businessmen, preoccupied with percentages and break-even points.

Outside the studios, people got excited about seeing stars. My young brother, George, fresh from Austria, came home in ecstasy: 'Guess what?' he said. 'Imagine: I almost got run over by Joan Crawford!'

To us insiders, the stars, big and small, were part of the scenery, day in and day out. Popular or unpopular, they were more or less taken for granted, except perhaps Garbo and John Barrymore, who fascinated everyone.

In spite of the fierce competition among the companies (you were a traitor in the management's eyes if you voted for another studio's picture at Oscar time) there was also a lively exchange of executive information: alcoholics or people regarded as troublemakers found it very hard to get a job in any studio. Warnings traveled fast on the bush telegraph.

This then was the microcosm I was transferred to from the sheltered life of the Shorts Department. Meanwhile, our first and only child – Tim – had been born. He was not too pretty at first, but he became a most charming child later on.

Kid Glove Killer was a police story with an offbeat suspense angle: the audience knew the killer from the start. All the suspense had to come from seeing him tracked down – step by step – by the crime-laboratory technician (Van Heflin) and his assistant (Marsha Hunt). It was interesting to see if suspense could be built up when the solution was already known (I faced the same construction again, some thirty years later, when making *The Day of the Jackal*).

The shooting went smoothly on a three-week schedule; the actors were excellent, especially Heflin, fresh from the Broadway stage. There was also a young beginner, Ava Gardner, playing a 'car-hop' waitress, who had two lines of dialogue. So unhappy was she about the awful job she thought she had done, that she wanted to go back to North Carolina immediately.

I used the crane a lot and felt pretty good about the picture. A few weeks later, the film was edited and ready for that awful moment of truth, the 'sneak' preview, undoubtedly the most excruciating three hours in the entire process of movie making, amply illustrated by Sean O'Casey's saying 'The theatre is not the place for a man who bleeds easily.'

My brother George, 1935.

Sneak previews were arranged without much advertising or publicity other than 'Major Studio Preview' and a couple of searchlights in front of the theater. It was the first time a picture was about to be shown to a hardhearted public who had no idea what they were going to see but, having paid for their tickets, wanted to be entertained; they gave not a hoot about the makers' sensibilities. It felt like putting one's child up for public auction. All the studio executives from L. B. Mayer down were present to see what they'd got, all seated well at the back, watching the film and the reactions.

There were certain ground rules: if a person in the audience coughed it was an accident, if ten people coughed at the same time it was an omen; if more than four or five people scratched, or whispered or jiggled about, it was a calamity; if they laughed at the wrong

time it was good or bad, depending on whether they laughed *with* or *at* what they saw; if someone walked out to buy popcorn or to have a pee, he/she was a mortal enemy unless they returned quickly. After the show, if the picture was very good, the lobby would be full of excited people rushing up to you, pounding you on the back and babbling incoherent and emotional praise. If it was mediocre, the lobby would be only half-full, with everybody standing expectantly still so that *you* had to move towards *them*, willy-nilly. Approaching, you could watch them trying to think of what to say. The comments would be 'Wasn't the photography wonderful?' or 'You sure got a picture!' or 'How about it?' If the picture was no good (a 'turkey' or a 'lemon') the lobby would be empty, with the last two or three people just disappearing around the corner and perhaps one lonely friend waiting to put a hand on your shoulder, look you in the eye, shake his head and walk away. Failure was worse than leprosy.

Preview cards were handed out in the lobby, asking the audience's opinion, and were carefully scrutinized later on. In Los Angeles they were mostly worthless: there were too many professionals in the audience and a card would read 'You don't need that dissolve in the second reel,' or, simply, 'It stinks.'

The story goes that, before the age of helicopters, Selznick – who, when asked if all these pressures didn't make him have ulcers, said, 'I don't have ulcers, I give them' – once took an important picture to Santa Barbara, more than two hours away by car. The preview was to start at 8.00 p.m; at 7.00 it was discovered that reel number three had been left behind in the studio. It was too late to change anything, the show went on without it – and the audience never knew the difference. The film was released without the third reel.

Later, important previews were moved to San Francisco. They now have them in Toronto and New York and the cards ask intelligent questions, but previews can still be quite misleading.

Our preview took place in Inglewood. The picture started well enough and the audience seemed to enjoy it. No one needed to have a pee, the laughs worked well and I was beginning to relax when, halfway through, I heard people behind me getting up. It sounded like a whole regiment and much to my bewilderment it turned out to be L. B. Mayer and his cohorts walking out in some haste. After the quite successful end of the show I was stunned to hear the reason: one of our best-loved stars, Carole Lombard, had just been killed in an air crash. It was December 1940.

Our movie was released without changes, to surprisingly good reviews.

A few months later Chertok and I started work on another crime story, *Eyes in the Night*. Not very promising material, it dealt with a blind detective who, with his guide dog, uncovers and destroys a Nazi spy-ring. I didn't like it much and remember very little about it. I hated the script but liked the writer, Guy Trosper, who also hated the script. The only pleasures were working with the marvelous Ann Harding and with Donna Reed, who was delicate and charming. The blind detective couldn't remember his lines and kept blowing take after take; the dog was good for only one take, would then get bored, run away and hide. The picture had to be shot in no more than four weeks, regardless. All this was most useful training for future occasions.

With a nice sense of proportion one of the critics captioned her review 'Dog bites Axis'.

The Seventh Cross
(1943)

Around that time I was fascinated by *The Seventh Cross*, a novel by Anna Seghers, who had escaped from Nazi Germany to Mexico. It took place in the pre-war years of the Nazi era and dealt with seven prisoners fleeing from a concentration camp, desperate to reach the Dutch border. The camp commandant had sworn that he would catch them and hang them from crosses put up in the barracks' yard.

Six men were caught, but the Seventh Cross remained empty.

The book was obviously written from close first-hand experience, in the guise of an exciting suspense-and-chase

Breakout from a concentration camp.

Spencer Tracy.

One of the seven fugitives, cornered, is about to jump to his death.

thriller. It had a number of important things to say: in a country gone berserk a man is running for his life, unable to trust anyone except former friends who are endangered by *his mere presence*. Forced to decide for or against helping him, most let him down, one by one. In scene after scene there are vignettes of human beings who reveal themselves under pressure. Finally, the fugitive is taken in by a worker, no longer unemployed and happy that the Nazi regime is at last getting Germany back on its feet. Scared stiff when he realizes the mortal danger he has brought upon himself, he does not abandon his guest but helps him on his way to the Dutch border. In a curious way the theme foreshadows *High Noon*.

I thought the novel could be made into a very good picture; but in the era of hate-movies it seemed a forlorn notion. Imagine my surprise when Pandro Berman, one of the best producers on the lot, sent me – out of a clear sky – a first-draft script of it, asking for my opinion; I had no idea that MGM had bought the story.

The book was great; the script was good, if sentimental in parts. It turned out that Spencer Tracy wanted to play the lead and had asked to meet me. One thing led to another and we went ahead. I learned an enormous amount about screen acting from him; he seemed pleased to be working with a young director and was most generous in support of me. Suddenly, I found myself bounced into the 'big time' – an enormous shortcut on the long road to A-pictures.

At that time Tracy was without question the most accomplished actor in the studio; no one was more greatly admired by his colleagues. When a signal from the MGM grapevine said that he was about to do an important scene all the young hopeful contract-players

would sneak on the stage and, lost in awe and fascination, would watch him from protective darkness. Not
that one could see or hear very much; he worked in an
enormously sparse, quiet and concentrated way and
with the purest economy of gesture and voice, but it all
exploded with energy when you saw it on the screen.
When asked how he prepared for a picture he would
say, 'I go home and learn the lines.'

He never gave the impression that he was acting; he
simply *was there*, always creating the feeling of truthfulness about whatever he did. He was the ideal film
actor and one of the two or three finest I have ever
worked with.

As a person he often seemed troubled and not at
peace with himself.

Quite obviously it was impossible, in wartime, to
shoot the picture anywhere other than on the MGM
stages and back lots; we had to simulate German streets
and buildings as best we could by rebuilding some
French and English 'city squares' standing permanently
on Lot Three. Fortunately, there were dozens of first-
rate German and Austrian refugee actors who had been
reduced to performing as Nazi thugs and who were
thrilled at the chance of playing human beings. My dear
ex-mentor Berthold Viertel, who lived down the street,
was immensely helpful in casting dozens of large and
small character parts, all connected by the figure of the
catalyst – the man escaping toward freedom. (Among
others, even Bert Brecht's wife, Helli Weigel, played a
suspicious concierge.) Outstanding performances were
given by Hume Cronyn and his wife, Jessica Tandy –
her first time before a camera. They were enormously
moving in their portrayal of a loving family threatened
by an invisible power. The picture was not as good as
it should have been. But it was nothing to be ashamed
of and in due course it led to *The Search*.

MGM and Berman must have felt the need to play
safe while entrusting a greenish novice with an important A-picture; there was a good deal of unofficial supervision, much more than I had been used to. First, there
was Helen Deutsch, who had written the screenplay

His picture is in all newspapers.

His old friend (Hume Cronyn) thinks Hitler is great, because everyone has a job now and Germany is back on her feet.

Above: *Jessica Tandy – her first appearance in movies.*
Below: *The informer: Brecht's wife, Helli Weigel.*

and was possessive about changing a dot or a comma; second, we had Berman's assistant, Jane Loring, who was on the set often; she didn't exactly get in the way, but hers was the kind of presence one could do without. The crew could tell she was a production spy, which was not good for morale. This being my first experience of the 'big time', I had no idea of how to deal with skullduggery.

Berman himself tried not to get involved and to stay above all conflicts, much like a constitutional monarch; but the most objectionable person on the set was his appointee the famous German cameraman Karl Freund, who had arrived in Hollywood in the early 1930s and had immediately landed a studio job. The story goes that, on the first weekend, he ordered his assistant to come to his house on Sunday to *wash his car*. He couldn't understand why the man laughed and walked away. (In a way this story symbolizes the difference, in those days, between Europe and the US.) Freund was anything but a friend. He was loud, slow and obstreperous; working with him was like pulling out teeth, one by one. To my enormous relief he got sick for a few days and the young and promising Bob Surtees took over.*

We young directors, chafing under commercial wisdom, looked up with awe and admiration to a handful of non-conformists. John Ford, George Stevens, William Wyler and Frank Capra had found it possible to defend their own personal ideas and beat the factory approach. Each man had his own guerrilla method. Ford did it with sarcasm; with one sentence he could strip the skin off people. There is a legend about no one daring to tell him that he was three days behind schedule on a certain movie; a petrified production man finally went to see him on the set. Ford looked at him with his one good eye: 'How many pages am I supposed to shoot in a day?' 'Four pages, sir.' Ford counted twelve pages in his script, tore them off and said, 'Now I'm back on

---

* Recently I have received furious letters from Germany, protesting about *The Seventh Cross* having been artificially colorized by computer, although it had previously been shown successfully in its original black-and-white form. The universal opinion seems to be that the colorization is atrocious and ruins the film.

schedule.' Once, when the producer came on the set, Ford sat down and began to read a newspaper. 'What are you waiting for?' asked the producer. 'For you to get off the set,' was the reply.

He insisted on sole authority. Finishing a scene with a famous macho star, he said, 'Cut–OK–print it.' The star said, 'I didn't like it – let's do it again.' Ford, who could be elaborately polite on such occasions, agreed. They shot it again and Ford asked, 'How did you like this one?' 'Fine, fine,' was the answer. Ford then asked for a pair of scissors, had the camera opened, cut out the large chunk of exposed negative and graciously said, 'You liked it, you can have it.'

George Stevens' method was called 'the Indian look'. After five days' shooting he would usually be three weeks behind schedule, whereupon the desperate producer would come crying on the set, 'George, the picture is out of control, it will cost millions, the boys in New York are very upset . . .' Stevens would just sit there and listen without any expression on his big, impassive face, never say a word and when the producer ran out of breath he would say, 'Thank you very much,' get up and go back to work. His pictures made millions.

After *The Seventh Cross* my relations with the front office began to run into heavy weather: there was a bit of unpleasantness and under some contractual duress I was bounced back to B-pictures and assigned to direct a child star, six-year-old 'Butch' Jenkins. He was a perfectly normal, charming little boy, who had no talent, could not remember his lines and hated being in movies, but was made to carry on by his mother, whom he feared and adored. Two pictures were the result and the less said about them the better.

I turned down the next script; a few eyebrows were raised and no more was said. Another script arrived, more dismal than the one before; I turned it down. A well-meaning friend, the casting director Billy Grady, said, 'You're getting a reputation for being pernickety, why do you have to be a perfectionist, why don't you just go ahead and do as they say?' There was a long, long corridor in the executive building – known as the 'Iron Lung'. Entering it at one end I would see the tiny

A disastrous surprise.

Tim, Christmas 1945.

figures of associate producers in the distance, coming toward me, spotting me, turning around and disappearing into offices, stairways, or toilets. I could see what Billy meant.

A third script arrived. It was lousy. When I turned it down, Eddie Mannix, the General Manager, sent for me.

He did not look amiable. 'What's all this?' he asked. 'You have no right to turn down assignments.' I said it was a bad script and I didn't know what to do with it. Mannix looked me straight in the eye and said, 'You know damn well that MGM never makes a bad picture.' Pause. 'We preview it; if there's something wrong with it we fix it.' To this day I don't know if he was serious, but I doubt it. Then he said, 'You could do very well in this company, you could be a good man for us, but you've got to learn to do what the boss tells you.' He mentioned the two least good directors on the lot and said, 'Look at them, they are the two best men I've got; they never give us any trouble.' I could only shake my

head. 'OK,' he said, 'in that case I'll have to suspend you.'

Stupidly innocent about such things, I asked, 'What does that mean?' 'It means that we stop paying your salary because you're not living up to your contract, and you can't work anywhere else because you're under contract here.' Bad news. 'How long does this go on?' I asked. 'About six months, until the negative of the picture you're turning down is cut. Obviously, somebody else is going to do it.' I was sure, without asking, that Renée would support me, so I said, 'OK. Suspend me.' Mannix, looking nonplussed, pressed a buzzer and in came Floyd Hendrickson, the head of the legal department, an extremely nice man. 'We're suspending Zinnemann,' said Mannix. Floyd too looked bemused as I went out the door; perhaps it was the first time a director had been suspended at MGM. The studio grapevine had been working overtime and, as I came away from the 'Iron Lung' back to the co-workers on the lot, I was surrounded by people gleefully clapping me on the back. It was as though I had just been honored with the Purple Heart medal.

Three weeks later Mannix called me again. He seemed embarrassed. 'I've been looking for an excuse to put you back on the payroll,' he said, 'but I can't find one, so I'm putting you back anyway. After all, Fleming and Brown [the top directors] turn down scripts too.' He was a rare specimen: a fair fighter.

Another director made that picture and finished it several days under schedule, for which MGM gave him a fat bonus; but the preview was bad and the director was fired the next morning. This may sound absurd but from the studio's point of view I suppose it was quite logical.

1938 had been a stormy year in Europe. In March, Hitler had marched into Austria, welcomed by huge jubilant masses of people. In September, at Munich, Chamberlain and the French sold Czechoslovakia, 'the distant little no-account country', down the river for 'peace for our time'. World War Two started a year later.

During the summer of 1938 my baby brother, George, now a strapping eighteen-year-old, arrived in Los

My baby brother; Versailles, 1962.

Angeles. He was drafted two years later and retired with the rank of colonel in 1975. Our parents, who had stayed behind, waiting for their American visas, were overtaken by the events and did not survive. We found out after the war that they had died, separated, in the Holocaust in 1941 and 1942 – two out of six million.

Almost immediatly after the end of World War Two, European film-makers began to deal with the shattering changes in their people's lives. Powerful movies, full of almost unbearable emotion, appeared in America from abroad: *Open City, Forbidden Games, Bicycle Thieves* . . . In Hollywood studios there was blissful ignorance;

the average 'product' continued unchanged, full of bland escapism and a sticky, unreal sentimentality. It was sickening to think of working on that type of material.

In America there was no clear awareness of what had happened to countless human beings in the rest of the world. No wonder: hardly anyone had yet dreamt of television, let alone of the direct, emotional impact of TV news reporting. American films could have helped, but the few great pictures (*The Best Years of Our Lives*, for one) were dealing mostly with post-war problems of *Americans*. Foreign movies could not overcome the barriers of language and subtitles.

We were as on an island of stagnation and claustrophobia in the midst of a rapidly changing world.

The Search
(1947)

In the midst of the flotsam and jetsam left in the wake of World War Two in Europe were thousands of starving, orphaned children; most had come out of concentration camps, having lost track of their families. Some were living in the ruins of devastated cities, with no one to turn to and fending for themselves as best they could. Gradually, they were gathered up by the United Nations Relief and Rehabilitation Administration (UNRRA). Some kids had forgotten their own language and even their names; some had become catatonic and had withdrawn into silence. In groups they were returned to survivors of their own nationality, who huddled in bleak DP (Displaced Persons') camps, waiting to be 'processed' and allowed to return home.

Technically, these kids were known in the UNRRA as 'unaccompanied children', an understatement designed to help the staff cope with the overwhelming tragedy and not be overcome by it.

An excellent Swiss film producer, Lazar Wechsler, who made a brief visit to the US at the time (1945), was deeply impressed by two things: the enormous generosity of most Americans and their total lack of comprehension of the depth of human suffering in Europe. He wanted to make a film about these children and, with the help of a famous war photographer, Thérèse Bonney, had been given permission by the US Military Government in Germany to do so. Having seen *The Seventh Cross*, he now asked one of the MGM executives, Arthur Loew, if he could 'borrow' me to direct the project, which as yet existed only in the thinnest of outlines. MGM was happy to be rid of me for a year; the feeling was mutual. I couldn't wait to get started.

It was clear from the outset that the story should be told in English and that one of the main characters would be an American soldier on duty in occupied Germany who finds a child living like a small animal in the ruins of a bombed city. It seemed a good idea to look for the right actor before leaving for Europe, and with the help of Peter Viertel I found a most interesting prospect – Montgomery Clift. We met at Armstrong-Schroeder's café on Wilshire Boulevard and it was immediately clear that he was the right choice: exuberant and full of energy, he was an electrifying personality. Most important, there was no danger of our picture becoming the vehicle for a star, as he was quite unknown to the general public, having only just finished his first film (Howard Hawks' *Red River*). Clift asked if he could see the script. I told him there was nothing on paper but that a Swiss writer, Richard Schweizer, had started work on a screenplay. 'As soon as you have something, let me know and I'll come over,' said Monty. Three months later we sent him a fifteen-page synopsis and he came.

Left: *In the ruins of Munich.*

Right: *A young actor still unknown in films: Montgomery Clift.*

Nürnberg. Adolf-Hitler-Platz und Frauenkirche

Research: the photos from here to page 64 are the result of two months' travels through the ruined cities of Germany and many Displaced Persons' camps.

Above: *Adolf Hitler Platz, 1938.*

Below: *The same square, after Allied bombing, 1945.*

The same square; Goebbels during a Nazi Party rally, 1937.   *Hitler's car at the same rally.*

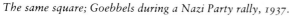

These two photos were given to me, on this spot, by a German, in exchange for a pack of cigarettes.

Nobody dreamt of doing films on location at that time. It was too soon after the war; pictures were made on studio stages and back lots, using exterior shots made by second units. It was considered outlandish to work in anything other than controlled conditions, saving lots of time in turning out the 'product' efficiently, as on an assembly line. We were one of the first Hollywood companies to break that pattern.

We had permission from the United Nations to visit all DP camps in Germany and to talk freely with staff and inmates. Once in Europe, it became quite clear that preconceived ideas were out of the question. These children had to be seen; they could not be imagined.

Most of the camps were in monasteries, convents and schools near the Bavarian lakes and even in former SS barracks, where we found a slogan still painted on the walls: 'Freedom means to *want* to do what we *must* do!'

Germany was then still off-limits to civilians; people in the outside world knew almost nothing of what had happened in Europe under the Nazi occupation. We heard first-hand stories directly from the people who had come out of concentration camps five or six months earlier. None of us could sleep nights because of the

diabolical things we heard every day for many weeks. It was pure Satanism; our brain cells could not grasp the idea of it at first. Stories were told without drama, in flat monotones. Curiously, not many were about atrocities; rather they had to do with the destruction of human dignity, the methodical tearing apart of people's souls as engineered by the Nazis – like forcing a mother with two children to *decide which one should survive.*

By now it was winter 1946–7. The children had been cared for over many months with utmost devotion by the UNRRA workers, and even though many no longer behaved like robots without a will of their own, they were still enormously disturbed and in need of personal affection. They desperately longed for someone who belonged *only* to them, whom they could call their own. When I came into a room they would climb all over me and hang on to me like a cluster of grapes, and I heard of one child saying, 'I'm nobody's nothing.'

Most alarming was the fact that remnants of various decimated nationalities were living side by side in some of the big camps. I had thought they would have been drawn together by their common experience; it was exactly the opposite. The Estonians would keep to

ENDLICH SEID IHR DA!

»Endlich feid Ihr da . . . «
ruft das befreite Öfterreich
den deutfchen Brüdern zu

Two photos from a German book.

Left: *Salzburg, 1938. Jubilant Austria, 'the first victim of the Nazis', on the day of the German army's arrival. The caption reads: 'Liberated Austria calls out to its German brothers, "You are here at last!"'*

Below: *'The day of joy in Salzburg.'*

Opposite: *'Peace for our time' (Neville Chamberlain).*

themselves, the Hungarians would keep to themselves, the Czechs would keep to themselves and there would be no middle ground – they didn't want to know about each other. They would cling to their kids, desperate to preserve their own national identity. All were victims of extreme nationalism, and yet they seemed bent on propagating it. It was as though they had been infected. Still, it is totally understandable when one thinks about their desperate need to salvage shreds of their own culture.

I was overwhelmed by the mountain of case histories we brought back to Zurich. Richard Schweizer, the writer, had stayed there because of pneumonia, and on my return I told him, 'I don't know where to start or what to do with all this – we have lots of stories but no central idea,' and he said, 'Why don't we make a story about a mother who has lost track of her little boy and is looking for him all over Germany; and the child has lost his speech and forgotten his name and is picked up by a soldier?' Suddenly it all fell into place, although Schweizer had never been near a DP camp. Then we chose a few of the case histories and used them as episodes on that basic theme, with the producer's son, Dr David Wechsler, collaborating on the screenplay.

It was most important to make the innocent American audience aware of what had happened in Europe, and for this reason we were obliged to soften the truth. Otherwise people would have been unable to bear it. The public was not conditioned and hardened then as we are now, and no one would have gone to see the picture. And we did want as many Americans as possible to see it.

The first part of the script was quite good; the second part struck me as sentimental. The 'American' dialogue was quite impossible; GI talk and behavior, beyond chewing gum or using the word 'lousy', seemed a

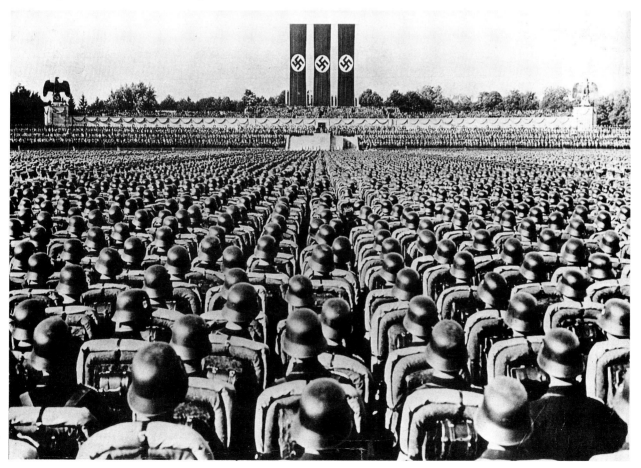

On the way to a death camp.

A permanent frozen smile. He'd been
warned, 'Smile or they will kill you.'

Leaving the Warsaw ghetto, 1942.

Right: *Nuremberg. War's end.*

Below right: *Former SS barracks, in 1945 made into a camp for 5,000 displaced persons.*

caricature. Later, Paul Jarrico was imported. He helped the dialogue a great deal; for his credit he suggested 'subtractional dialogue'. Clift's contract enabled him to rewrite his own lines completely, much to the distress of Messrs Schweizer and Wechsler.

It was an enormous challenge to persuade the children to act in the picture. I told many groups that we needed their help to make a film which we hoped would be an aid to children all over the world, but that this would involve reviving painful memories. If they wanted to volunteer, well and good: if they didn't, that was perfectly OK. They all volunteered. They were mostly Jewish kids by that time. The others had returned to their countries, but the Jewish children had nowhere to go. They became enormously tense and very, very upset when we started shaving their heads, putting the old concentration camp rags on them and photographing them with identifying numbers. At the same time we could see what they would bring to the film:

We had to shoot all interior scenes in a converted garage in Zurich. In one of these, Aline MacMahon, who played a UNRRA officer, entered a waiting room full of DP kids. We had only a small number of authentic DP children with us in Switzerland, so we took a few Swiss kids and I explained why they should be frightened of the uniformed woman. They seemed to understand me but nothing happened when we shot the scene. The Swiss children simply did not know the meaning of fear. They just looked totally blank. So I then took some of the real DP kids and all I said to them was, 'There will be a woman coming in, she's in uniform, and you think she is probably a German.' Period. Nothing more. She came in, in uniform, and the kids *were* petrified. They were not acting.

The same thing happened later; many children knew that the Nazis had disguised their mobile gas chambers

War orphans came from all over, having lived in the ruins of German cities.

Staging the film begins here. *The children's transport train arrives.*

The children are fed.

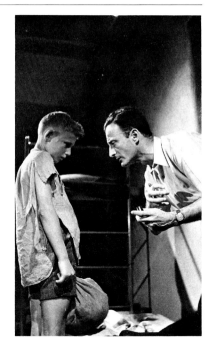

Above left: *Ivan Jandl, as the boy Karel, in the food queue.*

Above right: *Rehearsing with a surviving orphan from a death camp.*

Left: *An ambulance taking kids through the ruins of Nuremberg.*

so that they appeared to be like ambulances. When they were locked into a Red Cross vehicle during one of our scenes their hysteria was horrendously real.

This was also the time that Jewish kids were being formed into groups and gradually and secretly taken across the border to Italy. This activity had to be unofficial because of the still existing British blockade against Jewish immigrants into Palestine. The kids were guided by emissaries from the Jewish Agency, which later became a part of the Government of Israel. They moved down the whole length of Italy and were put into all sorts of small flimsy ships and boats somewhere near Bari. From there they made a perilous sea voyage across the Mediterranean and landed by night on the beaches of what was still Palestine.

Children escaping.

Almost all of the exteriors were shot around Munich and Nuremberg, where a German offered to trade, for cigarettes, snapshots he had taken at a great Hitler rally. Looking at the bombed-out wasteland that had once been the proud heart of the Nazi movement, he made a ghastly joke: 'We Germans are always fifty years ahead of the rest of the world – we've got our ruins now!'

One of the most important locations we needed was a river with ruins all around and a destroyed bridge in the middle. It also had to have a weir where one of the children could credibly 'drown'. Looking all over southern Germany without success we found it at the last moment, looking exactly the way we wanted it – exactly. We walked right into it in Nuremberg. (Those ruins of 1947 are now, of course, completely rebuilt,

but of cement instead of the great medieval blocks of sandstone.)

We had a tiny Swiss crew, no more than ten people, all of whom did everything. Time was of no great importance; our main problem was the difficulty and cost of getting negative film. If I shot more than three takes in a scene the production office made me feel it was a disaster. Our equipment was primitive and packed into one truck. Like gypsies we travelled in three cars through devastated Germany. We shot very fast, using many DPs in acting parts.

The Swiss crew was pretty stolid. They are a sturdy people and have great emotional stamina. By and large they were full of sympathy but were not bowled over as I was. They handled it well. We had learnt to control

The boy escapes.
Rehearsing with Jandl and Clift.

our emotions by the time we started filming; otherwise we would have been permanently shattered.

The cast was marvelous. Besides Montgomery Clift and Aline MacMahon, one of the finest actresses on Broadway, the child's mother was played by Jarmila Novotna. As the scenario specified that the mother and child were Czechs we went to Prague and auditioned a number of children and actresses. It was there I met Madame Novotna – a great opera star at the New York Metropolitan who had often sung with Toscanini and at the Salzburg festival. She was a very beautiful woman and consented to play the part without any make-up whatsoever. Approaching the part as an opera singer, a bit larger than life, she scaled her performance down and created a most moving figure. Just by luck we were able to get hold of Wendell Corey, who happened to be in Zurich on holiday and agreed to play a small part.

The boy is picked up by an American soldier (Clift).

We spotted the little boy, Ivan Jandl, during our trip to Prague, where he had lived with his mother during the entire six years of German occupation. He was nine years old, had been doing small scenes in Czech radio plays and seemed very promising. It was perhaps natural that he would not react if spoken to in German, much less speak it himself; in order to overcome his emotional block I had to work with him through an interpreter who was also his coach. Her name was Melanova and she did an excellent job, teaching him his English lines by rote. (Equally, when working with large groups of children – Lithuanian, Polish, Latvian – we had to work through their group leaders, who acted as interpreters and assistants.)

Ivan, now in his late forties, lives in Prague and is going bald – or so I thought, until I heard that he had died, alone and forgotten, a year ago. It seems that the Oscar he received had brought him nothing but bad luck. The regime punished him for getting a splendid award from the 'capitalist West'; they did not allow him to work in films and forbade him to accept foreign contracts or to travel abroad. Perhaps the idea of showing an American soldier in a favorable light was too subversive for home consumption.

Monty fitted in very well. His preparation was typical of the Actors' Studio 'Method', helping actors to achieve an unusually deep insight into character and teaching them the means of expressing it. He had not served in the Army; in order to prepare himself he went into the US zone of occupied Germany and stayed with a platoon of US Army engineers. The script called for an army engineer, so nothing but that kind of unit would do. One of the greatest compliments I have ever heard paid an actor was offered him while he was still unknown: when the film was first shown in America someone said to me, 'Where did you find a *soldier* who could act so well?'

As a person, Monty was super-sensitive and therefore

enormously vulnerable. It was as if he had no skin to
protect him. Beyond a certain point he kept his own
counsel, and he could be very devious if necessary in
trying to accomplish what he thought was right for his
performance. It seemed wise, sometimes, to let a man
of such enormous talent find his solutions in his own
way.

As the filming went along, Mr Wechsler, who was
guiding the production, became difficult and irritating
at times. The US group developed a compulsion to
discuss him endlessly among ourselves. It got so bad
that we made a pact: anyone mentioning his name after
dinner would have to pay a fine of five Swiss francs. In
my absence he decided to add narration to the start of
the film, in order to clarify the historical background

for the audience. The idea was sound, but the text
should have been better; however, it was too late for
further changes. Back home we screened the picture for
an invited, mostly European-expatriate audience. As
they were hearing the children's reports in their own
languages, one could hear in the darkened theater small
clusters of Hungarians, Poles and French bursting into
tears, one after the other.

The film was well-received, with excellent reviews
and important awards, including one from the United
Nations. The combination of non-actors and excellent
professionals had worked out very well. Back home in
Los Angeles I stood in the same old spot in the endless
corridor of the 'Iron Lung' at MGM; doors were flying
open, the tiny little people who had been running for

Top: *Primitive equipment. A scene with Aline McMahon and Clift.*

Right: *Jarmila Novotna, the mother.*

cover away from me a year earlier were now coming *at* me, all broad smiles, moving into close-ups and hugging me – 'We knew you would do it! What a talent!' This was when I became a cynic.

Ivan received an Oscar; so did Richard Schweizer and David Wechsler for the screenplay. But time was not yet ripe for a broad audience across the country. During that year nothing had changed in Hollywood, and after the depth of suffering and misery we had seen in Europe we found it strange to hear ladies talking placidly about re-decorating their living rooms and their new draperies. Also, people were under the impression that I was a *Swiss* director who had just been imported by MGM from Europe – a full nineteen years after I had first arrived in America. The MGM publicity department managed to convey the extraordinary impression of an anonymous lot of people thrashing about in a haphazard way and of a picture that somehow got made all by itself, without the presence of a director. The extract from *Life* magazine below provides an example.

MOVIE OF THE WEEK:

The Search

It is the realistic and deeply moving history of a displaced child

Displaced children are the most tragic victims of World War II. Metro-Goldwyn-Mayer's new movie, *The Search*, attempts to present in human terms the horrifying but impersonal statistic of 150,000 children separated from their parents by Nazi cruelty. Its example is a little boy who, after being torn from his mother's side in a concentration camp, is so overcome with grief that he forgets his name and even how to talk. Frightened of all adults, he runs away from an UNRRA center to wander among the ruins of a German city (*above*).

There he is found by an American soldier who gives him a home and teaches him English. In the end he finds his mother in an internment camp (*right*).

The Search was made in Europe with a pickup cast of both amateurs and professionals. Its forlorn hero was hired from a group of Czech choirboys. Many moviegoers should find *The Search* convincing enough (*following pages*) to cry about. Even the contrived ending makes a graphic point: as pure bokum, it highlights the fact that real displaced-children stories hardly ever end happily.

REUNION of boy and mother occurs by pure chance. Mother is played by Jarmila Novotna, Czech soprano.

Top left: *Novotna and Clift.*

Bottom left: *Mr and Mrs William Wyler visiting the set. Emil Berna is on the left.*

Act of Violence
(1948)

Perhaps the most vivid memory of making *Act of Violence* concerns the many sleepless nights we spent shooting exteriors in the eerie slums of downtown Los Angeles. The theme of the film – the fatal flaw in a good man's character – is best expressed in R.L. Stevenson's remark 'A man's character is his destiny', or, as one of the players puts it, 'You've done it once, you'll do it again.'

Based on a moody and suspenseful script by Robert Richards, from a story by Collier Young, the movie unfolds in terms of an obsession – a quest for revenge by an American ex-soldier, the limping survivor of an incident in a German World War Two prison camp. After years of searching he has discovered the whereabouts of the only other survivor, who had sacrificed the lives of a dozen of his comrades in order to save his own, and who is now a respected citizen in a community at the other end of the continent. The avenger – played by Robert Ryan – sets out to even the score. In the end, the hunted man – Van Heflin – expiates his cowardice by giving up his own life.

The actors were excellent; it was a special delight to be working with Mary Astor, playing an ageing streetwalker who picks up the exhausted, desperate Van Heflin running for his life through the creepy, crumbling night-time streets. A charming newcomer, Janet Leigh, played Heflin's young wife as her first major film role. Van, an old comrade in arms since the days of *Kid Glove Killer*, and the admirable Bob Ryan, were evenly matched; between them they generated a lot of tension.

The script offered a great range of possibilities for visual treatment; they were thoroughly explored by Bob Surtees, our cameraman. One of the interesting things about Bronislav Kaper's musical score was that it was conducted by a promising young musician – none other than André Previn – and played by the large MGM orchestra which, like all studio orchestras, was mostly used at full strength, even when few instruments might have been better suited; perhaps it was necessary to justify the large expense of maintaining it.

This was the last movie I directed for MGM, and the first time I felt confident that I knew what I was doing and why I was doing it. Personally, I like this picture very much. It would still be of interest to today's audiences, I'm sure – the theme is a permanent one – and I fervently hope that it will never be colorized, but will be shown only in Bob Surtees' masterful black-and-white photography.

Robert Ryan as the avenger.

Van Heflin and Mary Astor.

In May 1948 the British Mandate for Palestine came to an end. Survivors of the Holocaust were streaming into the country, which under the Turkish regime had been devastated by centuries of neglect and was now being reclaimed by earlier Jewish settlers. There was now a new hope for them which, at the same time, was a cause of enormous alarm to the Arabs. It was as if two people were trying to sit on the same chair at the same time, each claiming it to be his sole property.

No sooner had the United Nations recognized the State of Israel than the first Arab-Israeli war began. Enormous events were impending; after the experience of the UN Displaced Persons' camps in Germany I felt a strong need to witness what was going to happen next, and perhaps to make a film continuing the style of *The Search*. Monty Clift seemed to feel the same way and wanted to come along. My friend Reuven Dafni, then the Consul of Israel in the western United States, gave me the first visa and we were off. Joined by a talented young writer, Stewart Stern, we flew from Rome in an old DC-3 of Trans-Caribbean Airways, which was then the only airline available to civilians wishing to enter the country.

We saw history made before our eyes; we saw it but could hardly believe it. We saw Leonard Bernstein conducting a concert in Jerusalem, which was then under partial siege by the Jordanian Army (the Arab Legion) still holding the Old City. We saw Syrian tanks stopped in their tracks at the last moment inside the Degania kibbutz, which they had penetrated.

We saw the lawn of another kibbutz, Negba, the day after the long siege had been lifted. There, land mines were still being cleared and the kids were coming home after months of evacuation. During the siege the settlers had been under constant Egyptian artillery fire from a former police station – Iraq es Sueidan – a couple of miles away. They had lived underground, watering their common lawn at night, keeping it green as a sign of hope; the 'green lawn of Negba' had overnight become a national legend.

In the nearby Faluja Gap there had been a big battle; among the prisoners was an obscure lieutenant-colonel who became a historic figure a few years later: Abdul Nasser.

It was eerie to hear the Egyptian artillery booming away in the distance. Standing there at Nir'im one could not help but feel that in three thousand years nothing had changed, the enemy was still the same and the only thing that would ever change would be the cast of characters. (This was long before Sadat's journey to Israel, of course.)

In the end nothing came of the plan to make a picture. What we had seen was so much larger than life it would have looked like pure propaganda. No one would have believed it.

Israel, 1948. The former British police station.

The Kibbutz Negba.

The Men
(1949)

*T*he *Search* had made a fairly strong impression in Hollywood – enough for people to become curious about this semi-realistic way of making films.

Having finished the next film, *Act of Violence*, I decided I had had enough of the factory system and asked to be released from MGM; my old seven-year contract had expired, anyway. When this was done, my agent, Abe Lastfogel, the chief of the William Morris Agency, said quietly, 'From now on, don't accept any script you don't like. If you run out of money I'll support you.' And he did.

Months passed. At first I would get four or five scripts

Brando.

a week, most of them miserable. Then two each week and then nothing. After almost a year there was sudden news from two young film-makers, Stanley Kramer and Carl Foreman. Courageous and independent, they had already scored with *Champion*. They asked me to join them in making a picture about paralyzed war veterans. The very idea would have provoked a corporate faint at any one of the major studios.

In the outside world, next to nothing was known about paraplegia. Young men were lying in army hospital wards, their lives shattered, many marriages broken, many deserted by their fiancées, their children and parents now strangers, a return to former jobs or careers out of the question. Set apart from and almost forgotten by the nation they had defended with their lives, they had to face the fact that they would never walk again. Within a year many of them would succumb to decubitus ulcers and kidney infections. In those early months the wards were a chaos of pain, fear and fury.

At this point a new doctor took charge of the paraplegic wards at an army hospital near Los Angeles: Ernest Bors, then still an army captain, a Czech by birth. He was a urologist who called himself a 'plumber' – an impatient, irascible perfectionist, a medical Toscanini. With him he brought iron discipline and he struck terror into the hearts of patients, nurses and assistants. He was merciless; but he brought down the death rate dramatically and gave his patients hope. Today, aged eighty-six, he is revered by the entire paraplegic veterans' community and a new hospital building is named after him.

The patients were a cross-section of America: farmers, college students, blue-collar workers, white-collar workers, enlisted men and officers; their spinal columns were fractured, and the closer to the neck the wound, the more the body was bereft of movement or feeling. Paraplegics were affected from the waist down; quadriplegics – those wounded near the neck – could not move their arms or hands. One of them, Ted Anderson, spent a year trying to use a cigarette lighter. It was a great victory for him when he finally succeeded. (Two years later he managed to commit suicide.)

The ways in which the men were hurt ranged from the tragic to the grotesque. Ted Anderson had been hit

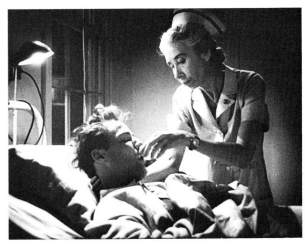

Brando and nurse.

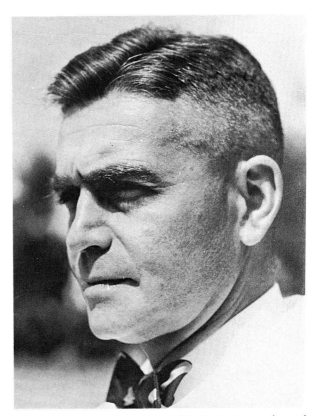

The great Dr Ernest Bors, Chief of the Department of Spinal Injuries, US Veterans' Administration.

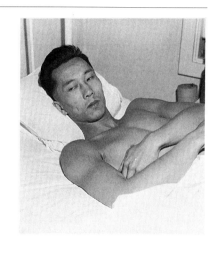

Arthur Jurado, Pat Grissom and George Iwamoto, paralyzed World War Two veterans, who acted in the film. Iwamoto was a member of the Nisei (American–Japanese) regiment, the most decorated unit of the US Army.

Convalescing patients try to cheer up Brando. Richard Erdman is the only actor in the group.

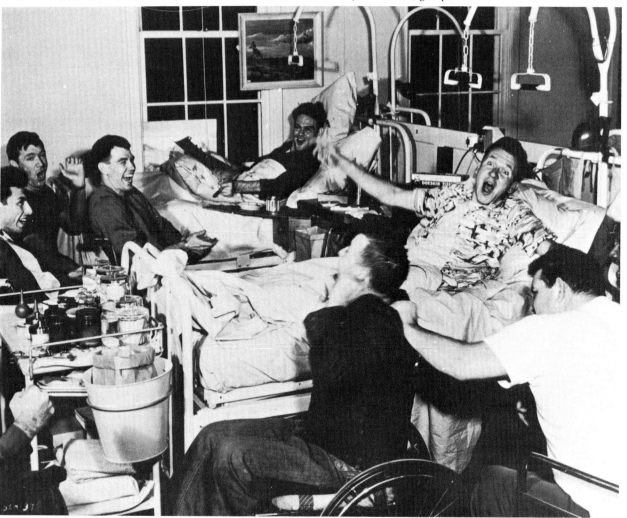

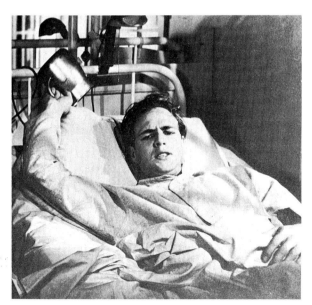

Brando insisting on quiet.

by a sniper while leading a patrol across the Rhine: he couldn't understand why he was unable to reach his carbine lying only a few inches away; then he fainted. He woke up five weeks later in hospital in Paris and found that the war was over. On the other hand, there was a soldier who had been shot by the husband of a lady he was in bed with.

Pat Grissom, a Kansas farm boy, was presented with a puppy. One day, sitting barefoot in his wheelchair he looked down and saw his toes covered in blood; he had no idea that his little dog had been chewing on them. He once closed an automobile door on his leg, not knowing that he had broken it. Herbie Wolf's problem was his mother: she was even more upset than Herbie and he had to keep consoling her. 'Turk', an ex-infantry man, once talked to me for an hour on the subject of pain. He said that in the early stages it was as powerful as the pain in the root-canal of a tooth, but spread over most of the body. Once he asked to have both his legs amputated to get rid of the pain; the doctors laughed and said that the pain was in his nerves, not in his legs – it would still be there regardless.

Dr Bors had a sixth sense about his patients. Often he would wake up in the middle of the night feeling that a patient was in a crisis; immediately he would drive to

the ward, saving more than one man's life in this way. His 'grand rounds' were an intense, dramatic and often funny event, and under his watchful eye the patients began to take heart; it was no longer the no-man's land it had been in the beginning. The men faced the fact that they would never walk again; newcomers seeing the example set by old-timers found things a little easier to adjust to; they began to excel in water sports and later on ventured into the world outside, including a bar called the Pump Room, in San Fernando Valley.

Before I joined them, Kramer and Foreman had already spent much time at 'Birmingham', the Veterans' Hospital near San Fernando, talking with Dr Bors and many patients. They had produced a very good first-draft shooting script; the leading characters were partly modelled on Ted Anderson and on Dr Bors, and there was a very important woman's part: a patient's fiancée who insists on going through with marriage to the invalid. The wedding night is a disaster and the boy returns 'home' to the hospital. It is the doctor who persuades him to try again. The end is a question mark.

In their newly established independent company the two picture-makers had already shown courage and imagination in their choice of subjects, such as *Home of the Brave* – a racial theme, quite controversial then and out of the question in any major studio. They struck

Teresa Wright as the pre-war fiancée who insists on marriage. Brando thinks it hopeless.

Brando, convalescing, decides to talk with Teresa.

me as being enormously efficient. Kramer was very inventive in finding quite unlikely sources of finance: he persuaded a rich lettuce grower from Salinas to invest in the current picture, to be called *The Men* (as well as in *High Noon*, later on). This method of outside financing from highly unlikely sources was truly original and far ahead of its time. Another of Kramer's talents was to organize very tight but feasible shooting schedules. His crews were always promised a small percentage

of hoped-for profits – a strong incentive for speed in production.

I was enthusiastic about this independent set-up and the energy it created. Working in a small rental studio near Cahuenga Boulevard, we were our own front office, responsible to no one for our decisions on screenplay, casting or production. There were no luxurious offices, no major-studio bureaucracy, no small internal empires to be dealt with, no waste of time or effort – and soon

The wedding night.

Below: *Everett Sloane playing Dr Bors.*

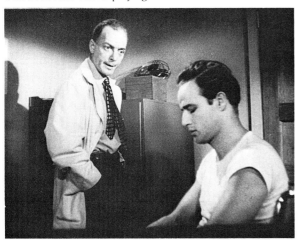

the time for casting was at hand. We were fortunate in getting an excellent actor, Everett Sloane, famous since *Citizen Kane*, to play Dr Bors; and Kramer persuaded the marvelous Teresa Wright, who had starred in great Hitchcock pictures and in Wyler's *Best Years of Our Lives*, to play the fiancée.

By that time I had spent many weeks at 'Birmingham' and I had a number of friends among the patients and doctors, including the formidable Dr Bors. Filming in the hospital was clearly impossible; in this picture the sense of reality did not depend on the locale, anyway. It could come about only through people – the people who had undergone this horrendous experience and survived it: the veterans. They did not need to act; they only had to be themselves. Their mere presence would force an actor to absolute truthfulness. But that actor would have to be exceptional.

From previous experience with non-actors on *The Search*, I knew that we could find enough volunteers among the patients who were not self-conscious and who would be entirely convincing; we decided to hold a number of group interviews and soon chose an excellent cross-section.

Now, for the leading part: the entire picture would depend on whoever played it. Kramer proposed three possibilities, one of them Marlon Brando, unknown to films, who had just triumphed on Broadway in *A Streetcar Named Desire*. We were in instant agreement about him; he was not only a great actor, but a shattering force of nature. He had a volcanic quality about him that seemed essential for 'our' hero. But – could one entrust the main part to someone who had never worked in films? Could he carry it? It was a big gamble and we decided to take it.

Brando arrived. He seemed fine, if a bit surly and very much on the defensive. It was obvious that he didn't trust any one of us and that he was determined to keep his own counsel. He was still very much the Stanley Kowalski of *A Streetcar Named Desire*, stuck in that character, and he brought some of him into his performance in *The Men*. (It was fascinating to see how deeply the 'Method' actors would merge into the characters they were playing and how long it took before they could return to being themselves again. I have seen it in

The final scene: Teresa Wright and Brando.

With Carl Foreman, Ted Anderson and Brando, who is about to re-enact Ted Anderson's war experience.

others – Monty Clift was like that, especially after *From Here to Eternity*. An interesting film, *A Double Life*, was once made on this theme by George Cukor with Ronald Colman and the young Shelley Winters.)

It took a bit of time to get used to Brando. Things were difficult for him and he was under enormous strain, having to adjust to the new medium. He tended to be ruthless in projecting his vision. And why not? People of such enormous talent should be allowed some extra elbow-room. As a creative person you have an obligation to be ruthless if you have an idea or an obsession you want to protect from interference. You can argue only so far, and if you argue beyond that you can talk your idea to death; these things are very subtle. You can start discussing an idea at great length and pretty soon it all shrivels up. If you begin rationalizing you are making a serious mistake, because so much of it is irrational and cannot be argued, like a lawyer's brief, on the basis of logic. If an unorthodox filmic idea is vitally important it is best to keep it to oneself and just do it when the time comes and not get into committee meetings about it. This may have been one reason for the frictions between directors and producers.

This was the way Brando prepared himself: he spent three weeks – day and night – living with the men on one of the paraplegic wards. He found out not only how they moved and behaved, but how they felt and what they thought. They gradually accepted him as one of their own and he became one of them. He shared their physiotherapy, played water polo with them and went to their drinking sessions at the Pump Room. Soon only a doctor or a nurse could tell that he was not a paraplegic.

The one thing the men couldn't stand was pity. They wanted to be treated like anyone else, not to be made to feel they were different. Pat Grissom, a man of enormous spirit, told me of the worst moment in his life: he was about to cross a street when a little old lady, full of sympathy, came up to his wheelchair, patted him on the head and gave him a quarter. He could have killed her, he said.

Sympathetic people often turned up in the Pump Room, even religious cranks – California is full of them – and one day a lady came in, already three sheets to the wind. She spotted the veterans in their wheelchairs, climbed on a bar stool and began to tell them that they could surely get up and walk if they only had faith in God. The fellows wearily pointed to Brando, who thereupon gave one of the great performances of his career. A tiny spark of doubt came into his eyes, just strong enough to get the lady excited. She began to harangue him in earnest; as she kept spurring him on he seemed to get more and more impressed. The room fell silent; people watched; the waiters stood there with their trays full; no one knew that Brando was not a paraplegic. Finally, he decided to make a try – and with a gigantic effort he stood up. There was a gasp and a hush in the room. People thought they were seeing a miracle; the lady on the bar stool sobered up instantly. Two waiters hovered close, ready to support him should he fall.

At this point Brando burst out laughing, danced a jig and ran out of the door. Soon he was back with an armful of newspapers shouting, 'Hurray, now I can make a living!' He did have a cruel sense of humor.

Two excellent actors were added to the cast: Jack Webb and Richard Erdman, and off we went. We shot the film in just over three weeks at a cost of about $538,000 – a modest sum, even in 1949. The pressure was, of course, enormous.

For the next few months I was away in Italy, preparing *Teresa*. In my absence, Kramer had shot some mediocre title backgrounds and a very good montage of Brando's return to the land of the living. I didn't have a chance to see *The Men* until the sneak preview in San Francisco – duly advertised as 'Major Studio Preview' but without naming the title of our film. To my amazement, the huge Fox theater in Market Street was packed to the rafters; people sat in the aisles and there was an electric buzz of anticipation. We were excited and bewildered: we had no idea of the rumor that the preview would be of Rossellini's *Stromboli*, starring Ingrid Bergman, who had left her family, gone to live with Roberto, and had been ostracized by Hollywood because of the scandal.

The lights went out in the theater and our film came on. When the title appeared there was a groan from the audience such as you have never heard. I will always remember Kramer as he turned to me, his face white as a sheet.

Of the preview I remember nothing, except my indignation at the kind of music Tiomkin had packed into the film – far too much of it and, on occasion, subverting the meaning of certain scenes. After the show we held

Tim, age eight.

a post-mortem outside the theater and I talked to him about it. I remember that he wept – real tears – but it was too late for changes.

The film opened in the largest theater in New York, the Radio City Music Hall, two weeks afer the start of the Korean War. Designed as a post-war picture it was suddenly facing a pre-war mentality. No wonder that people whose sons, husbands and fathers were going to fight could not bear to watch a movie such as ours. It folded in two weeks.

It was a noble failure. On behalf of Foreman, Kramer and myself I am proud of it.

Teresa

(1950)

The year 1950 was a Holy Year in Rome – an event that happens every twenty-five years. The great doors of St Peter's were open, the town was bursting with pilgrims from all over the world, ecstatic yet careful with every penny. They were looked upon with scorn and irritation by the Romans unable to make money off the *pellegrini* (pilgrims). One could hardly move in the streets; beds were scarce and hospices overflowed.

We were quartered in a Renaissance palace, once the property of Lucrezia Borgia. It now belonged to the Knights of the Holy Sepulchre (Cavalieri di Santo Sepolcro); to relieve the congestion they had converted it into a temporary hotel. It was a stone's throw from the Vatican and connected to it – so it was said – by an underground passage, now blocked up, so that Pope Alexander VI could visit his daughter, Lucrezia, in privacy. Luckily, I found myself occupying Lucrezia's own apartment. I worked in the huge living room and slept in her bedroom, its ceiling decorated with luscious frescoes, its window overlooking the Tiber. (It was

Teresa, a girl in a small Italian village which has just been taken from the Germans after a brief battle, 1945.

whispered that the bodies of her many lovers were eventually thrown into the river through that window.)

Five or six times a day, the door would suddenly open and a group of Monsignori would enter, unannounced and armed with opera glasses, wanting to inspect the famous frescoes. On the first day a maid kept coming in saying that I had rung and asking what were my wishes. When I told her, the third time, that I had not called her and that it must have been Lucrezia who had rung, a sudden noisy crack and a yellow puff of smoke came from the fuse box, right on cue. It was eerie.

All this was happening because Arthur Loew, who had been a staunch ally during the making of *The Search*, was eager to produce a film on the subject of war-brides – a serious problem which arose all over America soon after World War Two and lasted for several years. The war-brides were girls in England, France, Italy and Germany who had married US soldiers serving abroad during the war. All these foreign wives, who had been left behind while their GIs were sent home, were 'processed' and followed months later, landing in America in their thousands. Many conflicts arose when they met their new families, who did not always receive them with open arms; often these new relatives could not even converse with each other and strong clashes of alien cultures were bound to happen. Many girls found it difficult to adjust to their new lives. Some managed; others didn't.

Ex-GI Philip Cass. 'His occupation is running away.'

Loew's idea was intriguing; it would be good to work with him again. As the son of the company's founder, he was open-minded and relaxed, without threat to his job as one of the top executives at MGM. His life style was baronial; he came to work steering his own speedboat from a palatial Long Island home down the East River to Manhattan. Mooring at 23rd Street he was driven to his office in Times Square; often he preferred to stay in his apartment near the top of the Waldorf tower. (The palatial home unfortunately burned down a few years later.)

We agreed that the excellent young writer Stewart Stern (whom I already knew) would write the screenplay, loosely based on a novel by Alfred Hayes, *The Girl on the Via Flaminia*. It would focus on an Italian girl, Teresa, who follows her immature GI husband from her village to New York and soon finds herself in conflict with his domineering mother. There was to be an open ending – as in *The Men*: the traditional wish-dream of marriage as a guarantee of permanent happiness would be put in question.

Stewart belonged to the new post-war breed of screenwriters. He had a deep, compassionate insight into people's motives; to him, character was more important than plot or structure. Apart from writing the script he made other excellent contributions to the picture. In New York he had many friends among unknown young actors – including Rod Steiger. He was sent to Italy to scout for locations and to interview as many local actors as he could find. It was he who found the young, utterly charming and fragile Pier Angeli. Seventeen years old, she had made only one film, Leonid Moguy's *Tomorrow Is Too Late*. After I had seen her, Loew signed her immediately. It was sad to see her in Hollywood later, caught and ground down by the millstones of MGM.

In New York we next began the search for a likely GI leading man. Lots of hopefuls turned up at 'open calls' in a Broadway theater, among them John Ericson, a very handsome yet tense and troubled-looking young man. I was struck by his appearance, his behavior and his talent. He turned out to be a very good choice. It surprises me that his career has not lived up to his potential, owing perhaps to the negative character he had to portray in his very first introduction to an audience. (The film's opening line is 'His name is Philip Cass and his occupation is running away.') Perhaps it was something about the acting school he came from.

As a director one soon learns to observe the difference in the actors' behavior during auditions and to pinpoint the source of their education. 'Method' actors, for instance, appear – rightly or wrongly – to be quite sure of themselves and of their own worth; there are others who lack self-confidence and tend to be apologetic and to freeze when faced with a difficult acting problem.

Rod Steiger, the very essence of the 'Method' actor,

Opposite, top: *Teresa, played by Pier Angeli.*

Opposite, bottom: *Philip, played by John Ericson; New York.*

Right: *Soldiers resting.*

Below: *John Ericson and Bill Mauldin.*

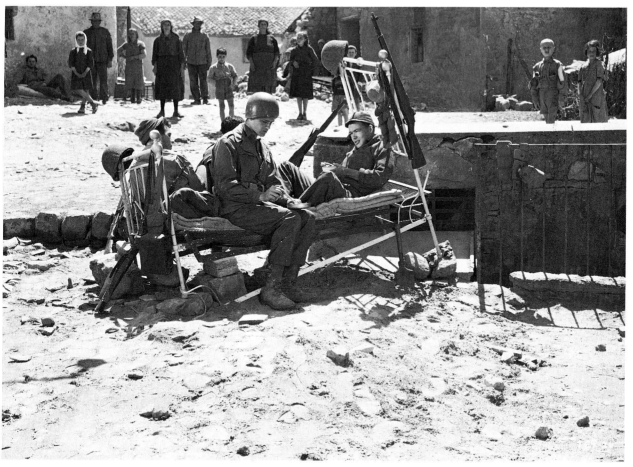

who had never before played in a picture, was very popular, extremely articulate and full of remarkable theories. His psychiatrist part was quite small; still, when his turn finally came he developed a block; he couldn't remember his few lines and was stuck – much to the amusement of the crew, who were behind schedule and under pressure and needed a good laugh.

When it came to casting the GIs, we turned to the young American ex-soldiers who, financed by the 'GI Bill of Rights', were then studying in Italy – medicine in Bologna, arts in Rome. Mixed with a few excellent American actors – Ralph Meeker and Ed Binns among them – they turned out to be completely credible in re-living their combat experience, with results similar to those in *The Search* and *The Men*.

In writing the screenplay, Stewart tended to dramatize his own personal experiences. This approach gave his characters unusual depth; in our case it led to an imbalance. There was too great an emphasis on a minor facet of the story – the mother's dominance over her son. Taken too far, it diluted the force of the main theme and weakened the 'hero' to an ominous degree. Bill Mauldin, the great cartoonist and ex-GI, who worked with us, tried to help with the script, but the start date for the Italian expedition was at hand before the problem was solved. My contract did not give me the power to postpone the start dates and to have the costly machinery grind to a halt, and so we committed the cardinal sin: we went into action with a script that was not ready and split in its purpose. And even though the first half – the Italian scenes – worked well, thanks mostly to the freshness of the two young stars and the exciting locations, the New York part suffered greatly. A charming performance by Peggy Ann Garner, the hero's sister, could not save it. It was a bitter lesson and one I remembered well on later occasions.

As we needed equipment for our ambush and fire-fighting scenes we placed ads in newspapers, knowing that in 1950, five years after the war, German uniforms and weapons could still be found in Rome. Soon, two non-Italian civilians turned up, assuring us that they could supply not only all sorts of German arms, from Mauser machine-pistols to 88 cannon, but even real live SS men (who were then still waiting for passage to

South America or to Nasser's Egypt), complete with their uniforms. Nothing came of it, although Mauldin and I speculated how interesting it would be to use live ammunition while filming – by mistake, of course.

In some pictures, as in *The Men*, the exteriors are, by design, only a background. In others, such as *The Search* or *Teresa*, the location is an actor, a dramatically active ingredient in itself. We agreed to shoot much of the film in the steep mountains between Florence and Bologna where the Germans had held the 'Winter Line' throughout the desperate months of 1944–5. The anchor was a forbidding, isolated mountain, Monte Adano, held by the SS. It took three merciless days of assaults by the US 91st Infantry, who suffered enormous losses, before the key position fell, opening the way for the final push down to Bologna and the Po River valley.

Villages throughout the area had been flattened and were now being rebuilt. Stewart found a tiny hamlet, Scascoli, clinging to a steep slope; we arranged to use it

for Teresa's village. The local people, poor and oddly submissive in the aftermath of war, were friendly and welcoming. The filming provided them with lots of humor and they watched our antics avidly: there was a huge, incredulous laugh and embarrassed giggles when the GIs were shouting the hero's last name, 'Cass', in one scene. It turned out that 'Cass' was the region's four-letter word for the male organ.

The wedding was filmed in a lovely, half-destroyed church in Livergnano, called 'Liver and Onions' by the GIs. It is not true that we asked for the completely re-built church to be torn down again. We had simply pleaded for a brief postponement of reconstruction. Final scenes were shot in Siena and in a lovely small studio above the Forum in Rome, as Cinecittà was fully occupied by *Quo Vadis* at the time.

It has been my good fortune to work with some of the world's finest cameramen: Gregg Toland, George Folsey, Karl Struss, Franz Planer, Bob Surtees, Floyd Crosby, Peppino Rotunno, Jean Tournier, Douggie Slo-combe, even Paul Strand – the list is long. People some-times wonder why I don't always work with the same person. The answer is simple: I find it important to 'cast' a cameraman in the same way as casting an actor. The style and mood of a film depends on it. Our excel-lent cameraman on *Teresa*, Bill Miller, had brought his wife to Rome from New York. She went home after two weeks saying, 'I'm tired of my own company.'

Our Italian crew was first-rate, enthusiastic, taking a keen interest in the making of the picture and applaud-ing the actors at the end of some scenes. Still, I couldn't understand why they seemed to be avoiding me in the beginning; I had always been treated as a member of the gang. Here, I would see two or three grips amiably

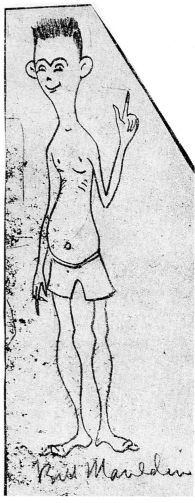

Left: *The famous cartoonist Bill Mauldin, our technical adviser.*

Above right: *Women of Scascoli.*

Right: *The* Queen Elizabeth (QE1) *returning troops to New York.*

The mother (Patricia Collinge).

The army psychologist (Rod Steiger).

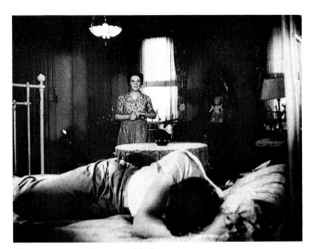

The mother and her troubled son.

chatting together suddenly freeze when they saw me approaching. One would say '*piove*' ('it's raining') and they would scatter in a casual way. When I asked Mario Russo, the assistant, about it he told me, 'They're afraid of you.' 'Why?' I wanted to know. 'It's your face,' he said. It took several days before I could come to terms with this revelation. I had always thought of myself as a perfectly harmless person.

Years later, when I was making my first picture in England (*The Sundowners*, 1959), I was flabbergasted to find myself treated in almost military fashion. People would come to attention when I talked to them; they stood up when I joined them at lunch. It was as though the brigadier had just come in.

In spite of enormous pressures of time and budget the work in Italy was a joy. New York was not, except for the final scene, which we actually shot in the maternity ward of the famous Bellevue Hospital. Eventually, production finished and the picture was made ready for the moment of truth: the 'sneak' preview.

After the first preview in Hollywood I warned Arthur Loew that we had lost the audience at several crucial points. I had failed to control the performance of the mother, the excellent actress Patricia Collinge. Her characterization of the mother was over-intense, draining the audience of compassion and sympathy for the hero, who was accordingly perceived to be 'wet' and sorry for himself.

It seemed clear to me that four or five vital cuts could bring about a great improvement, but Arthur had gone to a very good preview in New York, surrounded by well-wishers and 'yes' men who convinced him that this was a great picture. As proof for his feeling that nothing more needed to be done he sent me a copy of an enthusiastic cable from the topmost authority – Nicholas Schenck, the chairman of Loew's and MGM – together with Arthur's own comment: 'It is a pleasure to inform you that Mr Schenck considers *Teresa* an outstanding picture.' So *Teresa* went out with its faults intact, a lost cause despite some good scenes and the best intentions: a film divided against itself.

After many months Teresa arrives in America.

Problems.

John Ericson and a visitor (Marlon Brando) making mean remarks about the director.

High Noon
(1951)

Having read the first-draft screenplay upon receiving the offer to direct *High Noon*, I thought it nothing short of a masterpiece – brilliant, exciting and novel in its approach; I could hardly wait to come to grips with it. Friends were quite puzzled by my enthusiasm over what they thought to be the script for just another Western; but when I told the story to Renée, who is a good movie audience, she immediately said, 'You must do it.'

The story seems to mean different things to different people. (Some speculate that it is an allegory on the Korean War!) Kramer, who had worked closely with Foreman on the script, said it was about 'a town that died because no one there had the guts to defend it'. Somehow this seemed to be an incomplete explanation. Foreman saw it as an allegory on his own experience of political persecution in the McCarthy era. With due respect I felt this to be a narrow point of view. First of all I saw it simply as a great movie yarn, full of enormously interesting people. I vaguely sensed deeper meanings in it; but only later did it dawn on me that this was *not* a regular Western myth. There was something timely – and timeless – about it, something that had a direct bearing on life today.

To me it was the story of a man who must make a decision according to his conscience. His town – symbol

of a democracy gone soft – faces a horrendous threat to its people's way of life. Determined to resist, and in deep trouble, he moves all over the place looking for support but finding that there is nobody who will help him; each has a reason of his own for not getting involved. In the end he must meet his chosen fate all by himself, his town's doors and windows firmly locked against him.

It is a story that still happens everywhere, every day.

The scenario, ingeniously developed from a two-page magazine story called 'The Tin Star', presented densely compressed scenes of people in danger, forced to reveal themselves by nothing more than the exasperating presence of the hero (as in *The Seventh Cross*). The entire action was designed by Foreman and Kramer to take place in the exact screening time of the film – less than ninety minutes.

At this time, in 1951, the McCarthy era was at its height, bringing enormous pressures and anxieties to the unstable Hollywood community, raising anti-Communist hysteria to a point where people stopped thinking and became emotional, a prey to wildly exaggerated rumors. People looked at each other with suspicion; on the sets the crew as well as the actors were polarized into hostile groups.

The studios capitulated to the politicians. 'Fellow travellers' had to appear before a Congressional Committee and give the names of the people they thought might be Communists. If they refused they became 'unfriendly witnesses'; they lost their jobs and their films could not be shown anywhere in the United States. Many innocent people were persecuted and their lives ruined.

There existed an unofficial industry-wide blacklist; attempts were made to enforce a 'loyalty' oath, which many of us refused to take on principle. In the Directors' Guild things soon got to the point of 'who is not *with* us is *against* us'. The board was led by Cecil B. De Mille during the temporary absence of the president, Joe Mankiewicz.

A ballot for or against establishing the oath in the bylaws was sent to the Guild's membership, together with a strongly-worded letter from the board, recommending a 'yes' vote. The personal intimidation, such as heavy hints of unemployment for those who would not conform, was so intense that 547 members voted 'yes', 14 voted 'no' and 57 – including myself – refused to vote. Thereupon an incredible attempt was made by the board to frighten the membership into becoming a political instrument. A long cable was sent to everyone, demanding a vote to force the resignation of Mankiewicz who, in opposition, had uttered the word 'blacklist' from the chair. (See appendix.)

Fortunately, having discovered that twenty-five members *in good standing* had the right to demand an extraordinary general meeting, we took the loyalty oath in a group which included George Stevens, John Huston

HN-51

Talking about prudence and compromise, the judge has folded his American flag, and left town, leaving the Marshal (Gary Cooper) to look for support – only to be turned down almost everywhere.

and other illustrious directors, fully aware that the less well established and therefore more expendable directors among us were putting our own careers on the line.

In a memorable open debate, led by George Stevens and John Ford, our side won. The board was forced to resign and a new board was elected.*

Foreman's political position became increasingly difficult as the start of filming grew close. As the associate producer, he was forced to resign halfway through

* The best description of this important event is to be found in the book by Robert Parrish, *Growing Up in Hollywood*, published by Harcourt Brace, New York 1976.

shooting and to appear before the Congressional Committee. Shortly afterwards he went to live in England.

I was again working under the terms of a standard employee contract. The budget for the entire picture was $750,000, based on a gruesome production schedule of twenty-eight days, which meant that we would have to shoot completely out of continuity. (The first two days were in fact spent on the church scene, which is situated midway through the script.) As there was not going to be time for hesitation on the set, I had to memorize every shot and its exact place in the overall

His Quaker bride (Grace Kelly) decides to leave. (Photo: Marcus Blechman; New York, 1951)

picture; this would affect the building of sets, rental of props, hiring of horses and dozens of other details. Fortunately, from the old days in MGM's Shorts Department, I was used to 'making' the movie in my own head long before the actual shooting. The first image that occurred to me was of the railroad tracks pointing straight to the horizon, the symbol for an enormous looming threat.

In casting the main parts, the deciding voices were Kramer's and Foreman's; my veto was honored and my choices were accepted, when feasible. Jack Merton, the casting director, was most helpful.

We were thrilled when Gary Cooper, who seemed predestined for the role of the Marshal, accepted the part; the local vultures were predicting that his career was finished, as his last two pictures had not been successful.

Working with this most gentle and charming man turned out to be one of the happiest experiences of my life. Not once did he make an attempt to look younger than his years. Gaunt, somewhat stooped and walking a bit stiffly, he was exactly the right shape for the character. In spite of his arthritis he managed the fist-fight with Lloyd Bridges, the excellent actor who played his deputy, without a stunt double. When on location, his favorite relaxing position between scenes was lying flat on the ground, his long legs jack-knifed over each other, his Jaguar sports car waiting beside him. Audiences watched him as they would watch a baby or a white kitten on the screen; 'the camera loved him', the prototype of the vanishing American.

As the Marshal's ex-mistress, Katy Jurado, the fiery Mexican actress, an exuberant woman with a volcanic sense of humor and full of the joy of life, was an inspired addition to the cast. I was lucky to have excellent actors – Otto Kruger, Lloyd Bridges, Tommy Mitchell, Lon Chaney Jr and Henry Morgan among them.

Even before Cooper had considered the script his Quaker bride was cast, from a distance. The budget figure for the part was very low, but the role was not demanding; we simply needed an attractive, virginal-looking and inhibited young actress, the typical Western heroine. An ambitious agent from MCA, young Jay Kanter, came to see Stanley Kramer with a postcard-sized-photo of a very pretty girl. 'There's this girl playing in summer stock in Denver,' he said. 'She's done nothing except a small bit for Henry Hathaway. She's from Philadelphia, her name is Grace Kelly.' Kramer looked at the photo and signed her more or less on the spot. I asked to meet and interview her; Miss Kelly arrived a few days later and came to see me, beautiful in a prim sort of way and indeed seeming rather inhibited and tense.

Wearing white gloves, a thing unheard of in our low-class surroundings, she answered most of my questions with a 'Yes' or 'No' and, as I am not good at small talk, our conversation soon came to a halt. It was with a sense of relief that I sent her on to Foreman's office. She fitted the part admirably, perhaps because she was technically not quite ready for it, which made her rather tense and remote. The couple's great age difference, thirty years, worried me somewhat, but the die was cast. In the event, no audience ever complained about it.

Next came the job of choosing locations. I wanted a town in the middle of nowhere, with miles of empty space at the end of each street and a railroad track pointing straight into infinity. The art director and I spent a week 'auditioning' such tracks all over the Southwest. There was a great spot on the Santa Fé line near Gallup, but New Mexico was too far away from home; we couldn't afford it. Finally, we shot a large part of the picture in the standing Western street on the Columbia 'ranch' (the company's back-lot in Burbank, quite close to the Warner Brothers studio). There was one great advantage: the smog. It made the sky look blindingly white, just the way I wanted it as a backdrop, in contrast to the Marshal's black clothes.

We also settled for a fine piece of straight railroad track near Sonora, in northern California, and for a few street shots in the nearby town of – Columbia! Money was so tight that the set designer had to keep using the same wallpaper for any number of wildly different sets.

When it came to choosing the visual style, Floyd Crosby – a great photographer – agreed with me that it should look like a newsreel of the period, if newsreels had existed around 1870, which of course they didn't. In preparation, we studied Matthew Brady's photographs of the Civil War, the flat light, the grainy textures, the white sky. We put our studies into practice on the smog-ridden Western street in Burbank. (Each studio had a permanent Western street in constant use; I used it again, dressed as a Hawaiian street, in *From Here to Eternity*.)

Our approach ran counter to the then fashionable style of Western – the pretty clouds in a filtered sky, the handsome, magnetic figure of the fearless young hero. Our hero, middle-aged, worried and very tired, was constantly moving against that white sky. This upset quite a few people and soon screams of anguish about the lousy quality of photography were heard. Floyd stood his ground and never wavered. No filters, no soft-focus lenses for the actors' close-ups. He didn't change an iota in his lighting; no spotlights, mostly just flat front light. It took a lot of courage on his part; after all, he had to remember that it was not I who was paying

His ex-mistress tells him to get out of town.

His old chief says, 'It's all for nothin'.'

The town's banker tells him, 'Of course, there are commercial considerations . . .'

his salary. (Floyd had received an Oscar on his very first job, *Tabu*, which he photographed in Tahiti for Murnau and Flaherty.)

I believe this particular treatment to have played a large part in the effect the film has on the viewer.

A DC-3 plane took the entire company to Sonora, hundreds of miles away. The planning department and my assistant, Emmett Emerson, together with Percy Ikerd, had done a spectacular job. Taking off at 7.00 a.m., we were shooting just three hours later.

On that location something interesting happened to

Floyd Crosby and me while making a shot of the approaching train. We needed it to come from very far away, a tiny dot on the horizon, and to stop as close as possible to the camera which was lying flat between the rails.

Floyd and I were lying on our stomachs while most of the crew waited a few hundred yards away at the station. I gave the signal to start the train, and on it came. It looked beautiful, moving rapidly with white smoke billowing. Then it let out black smoke, which looked even better. What we didn't know was that this was a signal that the engine's brakes were failing.

We kept on watching happily as the train kept coming

His bride won't look at him.

A *funny idea, but the shot was not used, as it did not fit into the continuity.*

floating back down in front of the engine, which was suddenly there, roaring and flashing past and blotting out Floyd, who reappeared after the last car had thundered by, staring at the shattered camera on the tracks. For the life of me I can't remember how I got out of the way of that train. It all happened so fast there wasn't time to get scared. The camera was hopelessly beyond repair, but the magazine was OK. The film was developed and the shot is in the picture, black smoke and all.

The location went well, despite the enormous pressures of budget and schedule. The northern Californian countryside was ravishingly beautiful; it was great to be in the open from dawn to dusk. The training in MGM's Shorts Department had been an enormous help. Yet, in spite of all the planning, we did run out of time and money on this distant location and this pleased me no end. It happened at the start of a 'protection' sequence that I hated, as I felt it was not only unnecessary but destructive: it was a brief sub-plot located *outside* the town, dealing with a young deputy who tries to recruit help for the Marshal. This would have destroyed the unity of time and place which was so enormously important. Fortunately, we were obliged to abandon the sequence after two or three shots and we returned to home base. We never went back to those scenes and the film remained forever anchored inside the town.

When the picture was finally put together there were people, including Harry Cohn, head of Columbia Studio, who thought it was one of the worst dogs they had ever seen. I heard that Kramer had thought about selling the distribution rights to him. Cohn ran it and thought it was just ghastly. He passed it up – though I must say he saw it without the music. Years later, when Cohn and I were doing *From Here to Eternity* and had arguments and I wanted to torture him, I would say, 'Harry, you certainly made a mistake. You could have made five million dollars with that movie.' And he suffered. Poor Harry. It was a blow to his ego. He had a chance to make money and he passed it up. Of course a man like Harry Cohn, who had so many shrewd judgments to his credit, could afford to pass up one or two. If you are established and successful in your own field you can live with a failure or two; in fact it is good

closer and closer until we suddenly realized that it wasn't going to stop. At that exact moment everything went into slow motion: I saw Floyd rising and slowly, slowly picking up the camera and then the tripod's hooks getting caught on the rail and the camera slowly

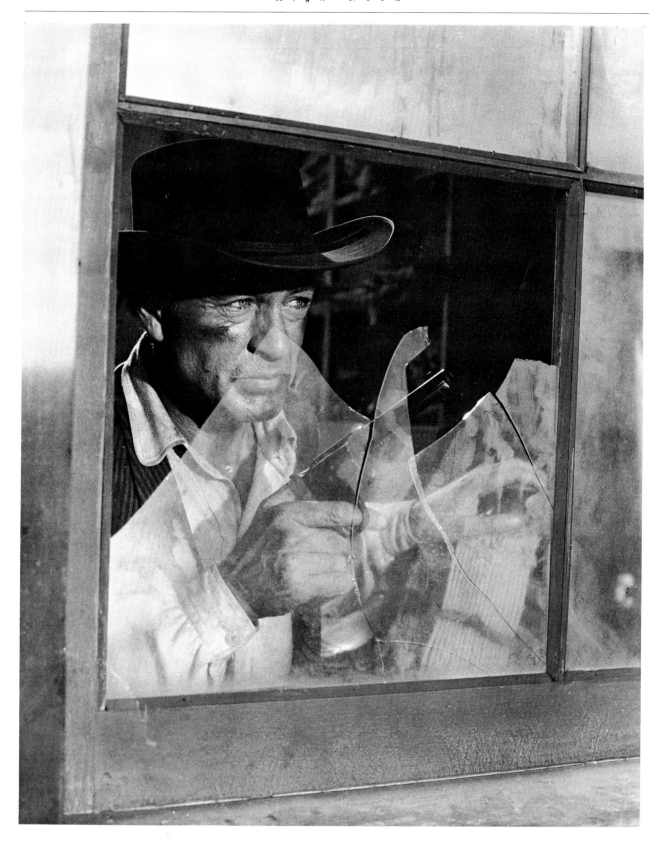

for you. At least that is what it was like in those days. Now, one single mistake may mean the end of your career.

Kramer had brilliant, original ideas about the musical style of the movie, especially the use of a theme song, which he insisted should be a Western ballad. He kept asking the composer, Dmitri Tiomkin, to try and try again, until he had come up with the tune to Ned Washington's lyrics 'Do not forsake me, O my darling'. This became one of the first, if not *the* first, song to be heard over the main title. Audiences, used to the sound of full-blown studio orchestras at the start of a picture, reacted rather nervously. I'm told that during the first sneak preview people were laughing at hearing the singing voice. Still, there is no question that the musical treatment – just like the black-and-white photography – added tremendously to the overall depth and impact of the movie.

At first, *High Noon* did not do very well at the box office, although Cooper's and Tiomkin's Oscars helped a good deal; it took a long time for it to take hold of the public's imagination. Interestingly, its popularity waxes and wanes; people become very aware of it at times of decision, when a major national or political crisis is threatening. Absurd as this may seem, during the panicky McCarthy era a number of people found *High Noon* subversive(!) on the grounds that the Marshal had deliberately thrown down the Tin Star, the symbol of Federal authority, into the dust ('and stepped on it', some said, which of course was not true). The Marshal's action was simply a gesture of contempt for the craven community. The nervousness about subversion was perhaps not even political, but rather a subconscious worry that the classic myth of the fearless Western hero, the always victorious superman, was in danger of being subverted. The Marshal was not *fearless*, he was scared; he was not a mythical figure – he was human.

Just the same, it is astounding to see how easily the mind can be bent to believe the wildest notions, no matter how irrational, if conditions are ripe. Panic of financial collapse, of unemployment, of inflation, of political conspiracy, can push an entire population into the most primitive and savage responses. All reason

Above: *About to start rehearsals; with Gary Cooper and Grace Kelly.*

Right: *Stars and crew lunching together (Floyd Crosby next to Grace Kelly).*

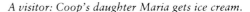

A visitor: *Coop's daughter Maria gets ice cream.*

disappears, and ideas that seemed preposterous yesterday can become holy gospel overnight.

Finally, a few technical comments which may perhaps be of interest. In developing the visual style I used three separate elements:

One: the threat – hanging over the entire movie, the motionless railroad tracks, always *static*.

Two: the victim – looking for help, in constant *movement*, black against the white sky. The tension is enhanced by:

Three: the urgency – time perceived as an enemy, shown by obsessive use of clocks (as indicated in the script); clocks looming larger as time slips by, pendulums moving more and more slowly until time finally stands still, gradually creating an unreal, dreamlike, almost hypnotic effect of suspended animation. Shot above normal speed, the buggy carrying the two women to the station seems to float by the standing figure of the Marshal. The climax follows in a fairly spectacular shot (impossible to obtain with a zoom lens) starting close on the Marshal and moving into the longest possible boom-shot of the entire town, the empty street and the tiny forlorn shape of the man turning and starting to walk towards his destiny. (We made this tricky shot with the longest Chapman crane, borrowed for one day from George Stevens. If you look closely you can see, in the upper frame, the Warner Brothers studio in the distance.) This was one of the few moving shots in the

picture; in planning the visual style I remembered what
John Ford said to me after watching my first movie:
'You could be a pretty good director if you would stop
moving the goddam camera all the time. There has got
to be *a reason* for moving it. Use the camera like an
information booth.'

My one regret was that we had run out of time to
shoot a *blank* clockface – without numbers or hands –
to be cut against a close-up of the Marshal at his desk.
It would have intensified the feeling of panic. (I had seen
that kind of clock outside Utter-McKinley's mortuary
on the Sunset Strip.)

One more comment on Carl Foreman's script: it was
constructed like a huge jigsaw puzzle, from a multitude
of small pieces; many of them were quite meaningless
in themselves, and they made sense *only* when fitted
into a precise, pre-planned spot next to other, similar
pieces. The story emerged in this way; the passing of
time was dramatized by the clocks which are seen in
most key scenes.

The construction of the screenplay happens to follow
the ancient rules of Greek drama – the three unities of
time, space and action. Each unity works only if the
other two are respected: if you were to cut away *outside*
the town, the broken unity of *space* would also destroy
the relentless sense of *time* running out; the unity of
action would also be diluted by creating a sub-plot
outside the town and distracting the audience from their
involvement with the main characters.

A year later, the city of Reno, Nevada, honored us
with their Silver Spurs award for the best Western of
the year, given to us as a main event in their three-
day May festival. Monty Clift stood in for Coop, who
couldn't come. The master of ceremonies was a young-
ish leading man from Warner Brothers, by the name of
Ronald Reagan.

High Noon *cartoons flourish when a national crisis looms
somewhere: June 1987, Poland's crucial elections; November
1956, Suez Canal invasions.*

Benjy
(1951)

Day after day the projectionists in major and minor studios spend long hours screening films – sometimes good, often indifferent or awful – rushes, assemblies, first cuts, final cuts: no wonder they are a cynical lot. Years ago, one of them at Twentieth Century-Fox said, after running someone's rushes, 'Hell, I can do better with an old whore and a Brownie camera!'

While Carl Foreman was struggling with the first-draft screenplay of *High Noon* – a slow, difficult job of building up a fully-fledged film from a two-page short story – I had the time to make a fund-raising documentary for the Los Angeles Orthopedic Children's Hospital, at their request and on a voluntary basis. I asked Stewart Stern to take part and in his usual generous way he agreed not only to do the research and to write the script, but also to function as talent scout and casting director. He wrote a good screenplay and found almost the entire cast, including the child who was to play the lead.

The story centers on a little boy, Benjy, whose mother can't accept the fact that he is a cripple, while his father not only ignores him but pretends that he doesn't exist. Only when the child hurts his arm does his condition – scoliosis, a crooked spine – become apparent to a young doctor, who persuades the parents and the boy to agree to an operation that will straighten his spine and make him 'normal'. In the course of the film many other children and their handicaps are shown within the hospital. (Today, forty years later, the techniques tend, of course, to be obsolete.)

Without charge, Paramount Studios arranged for the cameraman, Pev Marley, and supplied most of the crew, cameras, lights and film. We shot inside the hospital and Henry Fonda volunteered to be the narrator. Our entire production group worked 'for free'. Union members who were obliged to accept salaries turned them back to the hospital. Money did not come into this: as a result, all of us felt very virtuous. It was a strangely exhilarating experience for everyone.

The first sign of success came from none other than a hard-boiled projectionist who had just screened the first cut: he came out of his cubby-hole and said, 'Where do I send my money?'

It seems that the hospital was able to raise fairly substantial contributions and an additional, if unexpected, bonus was the Oscar the film received for the best one-reel documentary in 1953.

A Member of the Wedding
(1952)

In 1952 I had the great good fortune to meet and to work with three remarkable women: Carson McCullers, Ethel Waters and Julie Harris. There was also a marvellous child: Brandon de Wilde. This is how it came about:

After *High Noon* there was one more film I was to direct under my agreement with Kramer, who proposed a screen version of Carson's novel and stage play *A Member of the Wedding*, to be made for Columbia. The play had run on Broadway for about two years.

I had been very moved by the novel, a poignant story set around 1939 in a small town in the deep South. The writing was sheer magic: it evoked the figure of Frankie, a girl of about twelve – no longer a child, but not yet in puberty – living in a no-man's land of confusion and turmoil, no longer knowing who she is. Her old world – the kitchen shared with Beatrice, the black cook, and her neighbor, little Henry whom she bullies – has lost all meaning, and is nothing but a prison. We know that this state of suspended animation will pass in a few months; but Frankie's is a tortured soul until she finds the great, the only solution: she will become a member of her big brother's wedding, leave home and go with the couple wherever they go, to the ends of the earth. In Carson's own words the story is about the great American disease, loneliness; but it is also full of enormous love.

The great thing was that in the stifling claustrophobia of that kitchen nothing ever happened. There was hardly any action: everything important took place in the souls of those people. Given the public of the early 1950s this seemed to be an enormous challenge; as it turned out, the audience was not ready for it.

Carson didn't have much trust in Hollywood and was worried about the fate of her story. I was determined to protect it come what may and reassured her as best I could, keeping in touch with her while she lived in Italy and France. There was little time for the writing of the screenplay; I was particularly eager to work from the novel, as my ambition was to make a lyrical movie rather than a photoplay, and to preserve the magical quality of her writing – the curious, stagnant mood she had caught so miraculously; but the first-draft script did not work and as time was now of the essence, it was decided to go forward with the play. This meant that the picture would depend mainly on the excellence of Carson's dialogue and on the actors' performances. The small-town atmosphere would have to be caught, somehow, within the confines of the family kitchen; only very few location shots would be made.

I wrote to Carson asking her for suggestions for a well-preserved and 'atmospheric' Southern town. She mentioned Waycross and Augusta in Georgia, and Fayetteville in North Carolina; but it soon became clear that our budget wouldn't allow for such ambitious cross-country expeditions. Imagine our surprise when we found the solution in California: a small town near the Sacramento River, named Colusa. It had been built by Southerners shortly after the Civil War, and had quite a Southern atmosphere about it; it seems that there was great jubilation and a torchlight parade when the news came that President Lincoln had been assassinated. The citizens even tried to lynch the few Northerners who were protesting. This turned out to be a successful location with an excellent crew, headed by my super assistant, Sam Nelson, and a masterful cameraman, one of the all-time greats: Hal Mohr.

Working with the actors was pure joy and not too much of a creative effort. The original cast of the play – Julie Harris, Ethel Waters and Brandon de Wilde – had been together for a long time and they were in fact a close, loving family. Their performances had been conceived and crystallized in the stage play, produced by Robert Whitehead; my job was, in a sense, to transfer to the screen a work that was already powerfully alive.

Brandon de Wilde as Henry.

To Mr. Z,
from
Brandon deWilde

ALFREDO VALENTE

©D-8074-130

Julie Harris playing Frankie.

It was mostly a question of balance, of emphasis and non-projection, and of creating a mood of suspended animation around those three human beings.

Julie and Brandon were new to the screen but had very little trouble adapting to it. As for Ethel, she was so firmly wedded to her mechanics that she needed enormous persuasion to make a change (for instance, to take only two steps on some occasion when she had taken three steps on stage). Sometimes, when I insisted, she would look heavenward and say, 'God is my director!' (How do you follow that one?) But she was warm, loving and generosity itself. No longer young, she would sit in her dressing room between set-ups, sometimes humming softly to herself, sometimes playing records on her portable phonograph – her own songs, mostly.

Brandon, about ten years old at that time, was a lovely little boy, completely professional and self-disciplined and with a wry sense of humor; everyone was charmed by him. It was a sad blow when he died, barely thirty years old.

Julie, who was called 'Sunshine' by the assistants, is an extraordinary actress, one of the three or four finest I have ever worked with; at the age of about twenty-two she did the impossible job of playing a twelve-year-old pre-adolescent with such confidence that she was completely convincing, especially in her great close-ups, wonderfully photographed by Hal Mohr. (Hal was using new lenses, by Garutso, which gave enormous depth of focus to his shots.) I can still hear her reading the line when she was asked to play with neighborhood

Ethel Waters, as Beatrice, with Julie Harris.

children: 'I don't want to be the president of those little left-over people;' and toward the end, when she was beginning to appreciate boys, and a decrepit youth appeared in an over-large football helmet: 'He puts me in mind of a Greek god.'

Ethel Waters, with her mother-earth quality and her warmth and reassurance, was a rock of Gibraltar, a haven for the tormented Frankie. The end of the second act, when the three sing 'His Eye Is on the Sparrow', is one of the most moving scenes I have witnessed. (I say 'witnessed', not 'directed'.)

Julie was ferociously critical of herself. She didn't want to look at the rushes and was quite upset when she finally saw the film in a projection room. 'Is that all?' she said in a small voice, hunched into a miserable little bundle of despair.

Alex North had written a lovely score, but even so, the picture was far from being successful; in fact, it was a resounding flop, declared by the establishment to be fit only for 'art-house' cinemas. It was encouraging to hear a few dissident reactions: James Agee's, and the verdict of the Everyman Cinema in Hampstead, London, where the film had a very long run in a series of 'under-estimated movies'. It has always been my favorite picture, perhaps because it is not entirely my own – or perhaps because of the quality of pure love that seems to radiate from it so strongly.

From Here to Eternity
(1953)

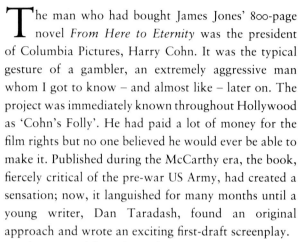

The man who had bought James Jones' 800-page novel *From Here to Eternity* was the president of Columbia Pictures, Harry Cohn. It was the typical gesture of a gambler, an extremely aggressive man whom I got to know – and almost like – later on. The project was immediately known throughout Hollywood as 'Cohn's Folly'. He had paid a lot of money for the film rights but no one believed he would ever be able to make it. Published during the McCarthy era, the book, fiercely critical of the pre-war US Army, had created a sensation; now, it languished for many months until a young writer, Dan Taradash, found an original approach and wrote an exciting first-draft screenplay.

Like many of the industry fathers, Cohn was a robber baron, predatory and cunning. Many people disliked him with a passion: some thought he was a crook. Be that as it may, he had no feelings of guilt. Where Louis B. Mayer was sanctimonious in manipulating people, Cohn never left one in doubt as to where he stood. He was straight in a crooked sort of way, and unbelievably rude. Meeting my wife for the first time, while I was away shooting, he opened the conversation by saying, 'Your husband is a louse.' (I took this as a mark of grudging respect.) Bull-like in attack, he even had a sense of humor, as long as money was not involved. In short, his was an endearing and stimulating personality.

Unlike some studio chiefs of today who need a computer and twelve executives to reach an *in*decision, Cohn was in every way a one-man band. In the very early days before I signed the contract I disliked him to the point where I asked my agent, the legendary Abe Lastfogel, to get me off the picture. Abe said, 'Of course,' to me and immediately went back to Cohn saying, 'Zinnemann is dying to make this movie!' – and the

Schofield Barracks, Pearl Harbor, where this actually happened on 7 December 1941. The victim was played by Alvin Sargent, who later, in 1976, wrote the screenplay for Julia, *for which he received an Oscar.*

Above left: *Abe Lastfogel, my legendary agent.*

Above right: *Harry Cohn, King of Columbia Pictures.*

Left: *A warning memo I wrote to myself after meeting Cohn.*

Opposite, top right: *Sinatra as Maggio.*

Opposite, bottom left: *Montgomery Clift as Prewitt.*

more I struggled to get out, the deeper I found myself getting in. Of course I found out about this much later. Abe was not out to make a quick buck from commissions at the expense of his clients' careers. Combining shrewdness with wisdom and a great sense of humor, he had a clear, intuitive vision of their talent and their future prospects.

It is necessary to see the making of *From Here to Eternity* in the overall context of the time when it was shot. The year was 1953, long before the Vietnam War, Watergate and the era of disillusion. There was an automatic respect for Federal authority. To voice doubts about any of its symbols – the Army, Navy

or FBI – was to lay oneself open to deep suspicion. McCarthyism was still very much alive, and filming a book so openly scathing about the peacetime Army (it was set in the months leading up to Pearl Harbor) was regarded by many as foolhardy if not downright subversive. Two studios had already shelved the project before Cohn bought it and he did so without even enquiring about the prospect of military assistance.

This seemed hopeless. In the circumstances I, as the director, became the focal point of very strong pressures coming from all sorts of directions. Jones' story dealt most movingly with comradeship but it also criticized many negative aspects of army life: officers abusing their rank, the brutality of soldiers toward each other, and the violent treatment of men serving a sentence in the army prison – the Stockade. There was also infidelity – an officer's wife having an affair with a sergeant – which would almost certainly not be passed by the Breen Office (where censorship was exercised on behalf of the production code) and even less by the Army.

The Pentagon's position was that no film based on

Left: *Bayonet practice.*

Below left: *Private Prewitt gets the punitive 'treatment'.*

Below right: *Drill.*

this novel could possibly benefit the Army, therefore assistance would be denied. But to proceed in those early days without the Army's help on technical advice, locations and equipment would have resulted in sheer caricature, with slouching civilian extras pretending to be professional soldiers. I was not part of the project then, but I would never have made the film without the Army's OK.

Fortunately the producer, Buddy Adler, known as 'the Silver Fox', an ex-officer himself, was able to win the military's cautious approval; they agreed to co-operate if two important changes were made in the script which was then too long by about thirty minutes. (Cohn had decreed that the picture must not run even one minute longer than two hours.) The first change presented no problem and was in effect an improvement. Taradash and I hated the second change, which led to

the worst scene in the film, but more about this later. On discussing our options, all four of us – Taradash, Adler, Cohn and I – decided to go along with the Army's proposal. In view of the Army's nervousness we knew that great tact and wariness would be needed throughout the filming.

Taradash had suggested me as director. He had seen *Teresa* and had liked the way the soldiers were presented. The military aspects of *The Search* and *The Men* were also a plus. Those two men – Adler and Taradash – persuaded Cohn to consider me for this plum assignment. I was still known as an 'art-house' director, or a 'director's director', meaning good reviews but no box office, so this was obviously an enormous favor. Cohn agreed, with some misgivings – he had hated my last picture, *A Member of the Wedding* – but he sent me the script. I was to see him the next day.

He and I clashed almost as soon as we met. I was given a vivid demonstration of how his manner could veer from the avuncular to the tyrannical in a split second.

'How d'you like the script?'

'It's very good,' I said.

'D'you want to direct it?'

'Yes.'

Cohn peremptorily mentioned an excellent young leading man: 'XYZ is going to play the lead.'

'Why?' I asked.

Cohn looked startled. Gruffly, he said, 'What d'you mean, why? Because he's under contract here, he hasn't worked for ten weeks, his salary's mounting up. He looks like a boxer, the girls like him. What else do you want to know?'

'I don't think he's right,' I said.

Pregnant pause. Then Cohn asked, 'Who is it *you* want?'

'Montgomery Clift.'

That was when Cohn became very angry indeed. The sense of his tirade was that this was an idiotic suggestion. Clift was wrong for the part of Prewitt (the young army private who refuses to box for his company and has his life made hell by his glory-hunting captain). He was no soldier and no boxer and probably a homosexual, said Cohn.

Donna Reed playing Lorene, the nightclub princess.

The first paragraph in Jones' book describes Prewitt as a 'deceptively slim young man'. It was just that quality, the 'deceptive slimness', I needed to give an edge to Prewitt's character. I wanted Clift because this story was not about a fellow who didn't want to box: it was about the human spirit refusing to be broken, about a man who resists all sorts of pressure from an institution he loves, who becomes an outsider, and eventually dies for it. It was quite clear to me, if difficult to explain, what Clift would make of that character.

Finally, Cohn said, 'I'm the president of Columbia. You can't give me ultimatums,' and I told him that I couldn't do justice to the script unless I felt confident that I had the right cast, and perhaps he should get another director. Thanking him for his interest, I left him screaming (it was Cohn who was screaming); but he did send the script to Clift the next day.

So, we started our working relationship on the basis of mutual hatred, mixed with mutual respect. Cohn wasn't quite sure what to make of me; and in turn, I grew to appreciate his sense of showmanship and his predicament: he ran his company like a medieval fiefdom, by sheer terror; he had spies on every set and he knew everything that was going on in the studio –

who was sending whom flowers, who was sleeping with whom; he knew it all and people 'yessed' him day in day out. ('Why don't you let me finish before you say yes?' as C. B. De Mille once said.) Yet, in rare moments of repose, his eyes were sad; he seemed a man in search of people who would say 'No' to him and mean it.

Clift rose brilliantly to the occasion. He didn't know how to box, much less how to play the bugle, and he certainly knew nothing about close-order drill; there were long sessions with one of the great bugle players, Manny Kline, and endless hours of bayonet practice at Schofield Barracks in Honolulu, where much of the picture was shot. By the time Monty was ready for the cameras one could have sworn that he had bugled all his life and that he was a top soldier AND a good boxer. In the very first shot behind the credit titles he was introduced as a loner, going his own way – a tiny figure approaching the camera, growing larger and larger, seen through an infantry platoon moving across the screen in the foreground.

For many months after the end of filming Monty continued to be possessed by his own creation – Private Prewitt. He was quite unable to get out of that character. By his intensity he forced the other actors to come up to his standard of performance. But casting *From Here to Eternity* was a question of getting not only the right person for the right part, but the chemistry between the actors – how they would work together.

Most people had thought of Joan Crawford for the part of Karen – the captain's adulterous wife. She seemed adequate, but I had nagging doubts, knowing that she had already started discussing her wardrobe. Then suddenly the agent Bert Allenberg – a man with the rare talent of reading letters upside down – phoned.

He sounded diffident. 'What about Deborah Kerr?' he asked. Dan, Buddy and I thought casting *against type* a brilliant idea. Up to that point Miss Kerr had played ladies who had what Hollywood calls 'class', and rather chilly class at that. (When posing in a swimsuit for wardrobe stills, she was heard to say, 'I feel naked without my tiara.') I thought that, hearing a corporal say at the start of the film that 'she sleeps with every soldier on the post', the audience would *not* believe it. They would be curious to see how things would develop,

Deborah Kerr and Burt Lancaster, rehearsing dialogue lines with coach Jus Addis.

so the casting of Deborah would create an added sense of suspense and excitement. If a sexy actress were to play that part the outcome would be a foregone conclusion. Cohn could see the showmanship in it: he didn't need persuading. Nor, as it happened, did Deborah. Her performance opened a whole new range of roles for her.

Burt Lancaster seemed to be the best choice for the part of the master sergeant. This *was* type-casting. Not only did he have the right authority and weight, but more importantly there was a chemistry between him and Deborah, and the combination worked out well, especially in the beach scene, which we shot near

Diamond Head, close to Honolulu, in the course of our three weeks' location there. The challenge was timing the scene with the incoming waves so that they would break over the couple at the right instant. (Typically, Cohn had demanded shooting to begin immediately upon arrival after the night flight from Los Angeles; but we just didn't do it.)

That scene, regarded as sensational and extremely provocative a mere twenty-five years ago, seems harmless and friendly by today's standards. Although it was shot very much as written, the movie censors, who knew the script by heart, nevertheless insisted on deleting four seconds of it. In later years I found that even more had been snipped out by theater projectionists, as a souvenir no doubt. For many years the tourist buses used to stop routinely at this point on the Hawaiian shoreline to let people admire 'the spot where Burt and Deborah made love in the waves'. It is a curious contribution we have made to popular culture.

Two important roles were still open. One was that of Lorene, the small-town girl from Iowa who works in a Hawaiian brothel. Because of censorship, in Dan Taradash's script the brothel had been converted into a club and the girl into a hostess. Lorene, born poor, on the wrong side of the railroad tracks, has only one ambition: to make enough money to return to her home

The captain's wife.

town and be proper and respectable; a bourgeois ideal, used with brilliant irony by the author. Donna Reed was not my first choice, but one could not forever say 'No' to Cohn. Lorene was called 'the princess' by the other girls and Donna fitted that description. Besides, she was under contract to Columbia. She got the part, and played it so touchingly and so well that an Oscar was her reward.

Last but not least was the part of Maggio, Prewitt's

friend, the army rebel who gets slung into the Stockade, where brutal punishment breaks his body, if not his spirit, and causes his death in Prewitt's arms. I had wanted Eli Wallach, who had made an excellent test, but I understood that Kazan needed him to fulfil his earlier promise to be in *Camino Real*, on Broadway. (The other story I heard was that Eli Wallach's agent wanted too much money.) The man who was determined to get the part redoubled his efforts: it was none other than Frank Sinatra, who had read the script and bombarded all of us – Cohn, Adler and myself – with pleading cables all signed 'Maggio'. His career was in the doldrums then but in spite of one or two unsuccessful pictures he seemed a possibility, although Cohn doubted it.

Sinatra was in Africa, where Ava Gardner was filming *Mogambo*, when Cohn, always careful with money, cabled him that a test could be made if he would pay his own way back to Hollywood. In a flash, Sinatra had returned and the test turned out well – it was Sinatra in uniform. Cohn paid him a bare $8,000 for the part – but this was a turning point for Sinatra; he received an Oscar, and from then on his career took off like a rocket. At no time were horses' heads involved in the casting decision. The author of *The Godfather* was using poetic license.

Sinatra was at his best in the first or second take of a scene: in later takes he was apt to lose spontaneity, whereas Clift would use each take as a rehearsal to add more detail so that the scenes gained in depth as we went on. It was an interesting problem when they did a scene together: how to get the best performance from them both in the same take. With due respect it reminded me of the situation in one of my earliest films, *Eyes in the Night*, where a blind detective needed eight takes before he could remember his lines; his bored guide dog would run away and hide after the first take.

We had excellent co-operation from the Army in Hawaii: our technical adviser, Bill Mullen, a tough military police sergeant, was very good on drill and proper military bearing. The commanding general, known affectionately as 'Iron-Ass Mike', by strange irony

Extract from Look *magazine.*

CENSORED

Preferring self-regulation to intervention, Hollywood submits movie scripts, film and still photographs for approval to the Association of Motion Picture Producers, better known after its chief as the Breen Office. A sequence played by usually decorous Deborah Kerr and always agile Burt Lancaster in *From Here to Eternity* was thus censored. With mysterious logic, the Breen Office decreed that the stills shown on the next page were not to be used for publicity, advertising or other purposes. What was objected to, according to reports, was the water.

41

End

Bar scenes – work photos.

Sinatra's death scene.

looked not unlike Harry Cohn! Cohn himself left us alone; he was in residence at the Royal Hawaiian Hotel but kept getting minute-by-minute reports from his various spies.

One of the last location scenes to be shot in Hawaii was a night exterior – Maggio's arrest by the military police. Maggio, blind drunk along with Prewitt in a Honolulu park, feels harassed beyond endurance; his rage boils over, he *jumps up*, berating the policemen, who are twice his size, and attacks them.

The afternoon's rehearsal was excellent, but Cohn had heard about it and thought that we would be in trouble with the Army – Sinatra was just too provocative. He wanted us to tone things down; the actors and I disagreed with this view, although I felt the objection had come from someone outside, above Cohn.

For a few mad hours I believed that I could get away with shooting the scene as rehearsed and presenting Cohn with an accomplished fact. Night fell; lights and camera were ready. Cohn was not present, but his informers were. At the last moment, he roared up to the set, together with the garrison's top echelon of officers. They had come ostensibly to watch us at work but it soon became clear that a confrontation could develop and lead to closing down the picture. We were,

after all, on army territory. I knew that we could be jeopardizing the whole film; it was a situation I could not win. To quit was out of the question as far as I was concerned.

Sinatra delivered his speech while *seated*. I can't blame him for being upset; but I wonder whether he ever understood what was at stake.

The first Army-imposed script change was actually an improvement: nothing should be shown of the brutal treatment meted out to Maggio inside the Stockade, at the mercy of the sadistic sergeant (Ernest Borgnine). This was fine with me: Sinatra's death scene in Prewitt's arms would tell it all. At the end of the scene when his limp body is put into the jeep, Clift originally said, 'See that his head don't bump.' That powerful emotional moment was cut. Cohn was adamant that the film should not run a minute longer than two hours; contractually it was he who had the 'final cut'. I had no recourse.

The second script change eliminated a splendid sarcastic touch at the end of the novel: the promotion of

Knife-fight. Clift and Ernest Borgnine.

Schofield Barracks, Pearl Harbor. Several US Air Force training planes were repainted to look like Japanese Zeros.

the villainous captain to the rank of major. The Army would have none of that. It was one of the two basic conditions for their co-operation: the captain should be found out and given the choice of resigning from the Army or facing a court martial. It led to the worst moment in the film, resembling a recruiting short. It makes me sick every time I see it. Today, most of the sardonic comments of the novel could be filmed without much trouble; to have tried using them in 1953 would have meant giving up the film altogether.

In retrospect, I am surprised to think how many battles I did win during the making of the film. One of them had to do with color: the sales department ('the boys in New York') made it plain that the film would gross an extra million if it was shot in color, but I was able to persuade Cohn to agree to making it in

black-and-white. This made a great difference; color would have made the movie look soft and trivial.

Thanks to the enormous help from Buddy Adler and to the excellent production crew the picture was shot in forty-one days, including the Hawaiian location. We started filming in early March and finished in May. Three months later the picture was in the theaters.

The first preview had happened much earlier and was conducted in an unorthodox way. Cohn had decided to use a new electronic system of recording audience reactions. About two hundred people were, literally, wired to their seats in a large projection room. There were small levers each could push – to the right if they liked the scene, to the left if they didn't. At first this seemed a ridiculous enterprise, especially discouraging because there was absolutely no reaction from the

Discussing a scene with Clift and Sinatra.

For months on end there was no time for a haircut.

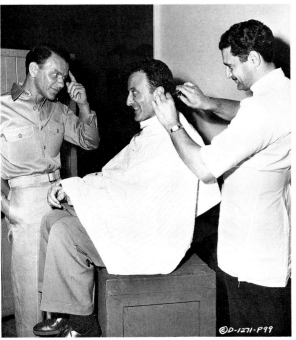

audience. They sat there like wax figures at Madame Tussauds, busy concentrating on those levers. I was convinced we had a disaster on our hands.

Then Harry Cohn came tearing in, carrying a roll of paper twenty-five feet long, with the combined graph of those two hundred people plotted on it, and he said excitedly that the curve indicated Columbia was going to have its biggest-ever hit. The curve, he said, showed not only what people had enjoyed but *how much* they had enjoyed it, and it also showed the slow spots. It was eerie to see human reactions reduced to this twenty-five-foot roll of paper. But even worse, it worked – and was used for quite some time afterwards.

There was no time and no need to make changes after that preview but we all thought Cohn had gone mad when he decreed that 'this picture will open in the Capitol Theater on Broadway in New York in August'. There was no air-conditioning then, and in August New York was a sweatbox. No one had ever heard of releasing a major film in mid-summer. We were convinced that his gambler's instinct was leading to certain suicide. More was to come: Cohn declared that there would be no publicity, except for one full-page ad in the *Times* which *he* would sign as president of Columbia, urging people to see it.

I was in Los Angeles when the picture opened on Broadway, on a sweltering August night. No première, no limousines, nothing. At 9.00 p.m., Marlene Dietrich (whom I hardly knew) called from New York and said that it was midnight there but the Capitol Theater was bulging, people were still standing around the block and there was an extra performance starting at one in the morning! I said, 'How is that possible? There has been no publicity.' – 'They smell it,' she said.

That year there was stiff competition for Oscars. Willie Wyler had *Roman Holiday*, George Stevens had *Shane*, Billy Wilder had *Stalag 17*. I was encouraged to see that we had thirteen nominations, including an incredible one for *costumes*, which consisted largely of uniforms and a bikini for Deborah; judging by this straw in the wind, it seemed to me that we were in for a wave of popular approval. We did in fact get eight Oscars on that occasion, not, to my great regret, including Deborah and Monty.

Marlon Brando visiting.

Thirteen nominations and eight Oscars. Bernie Guffey (camera), Dan Taradash (script), Donna Reed, me, Buddy Adler (producer). (Sinatra, editor Bill Lyons and sound man L. Cunningham were missing.)

Cohn had an incredible knack for saving an extra penny. Dan Taradash and I were working with him on cutting the dialogue one evening; it was 8.00 p.m., I had laryngitis and wanted to go home. 'No, no,' Cohn said, 'we've got to finish this tonight. I'll take you to dinner at Perrino's [the poshest restaurant in Los Angeles at that time] and then we'll come back here.' I said I had no necktie. Cohn snorted, pressed a button and a poor man from the wardrobe department appeared, trembling. He had never been in the Presence before and couldn't imagine what crime he might have committed to be summoned at this time of night. 'Bring three ties,' Cohn growled. The man came back with three cheesy ones, worth about seventy-five cents each, and I picked one. We returned after a good dinner and worked away until midnight. As I was walking out of the door Cohn said, 'Hey, wait a minute, give me back that tie!' Imagine a man about to spend two million dollars on a movie keeping a beady eye on a seventy-five-cent tie!

As to Cohn's showmanship, he paid little attention to thirty of the thirty-two pictures the studio turned out each year, but took enormous pride in one or two special movies such as *From Here to Eternity*. His taste was quite often awful, but he had huge experience and a gut instinct about audiences and he constantly got into our hair checking every line of dialogue, worrying about casting, wardrobe and locations. But he loved movies. I wish there were more studio heads like him today.

Oklahoma!
(1954–1955)

Panic stations.

After *From Here to Eternity* and the Oscars, I was suddenly propelled into the big league. As if by magic the whole scene had changed. Some things were pleasant and most people were charming but I had seen life from the worm's perspective long enough to sense what was phony and what wasn't. There was a whole set of fair-weather friends, unlimited vistas, wider horizons, great politeness and *no* resistance from front offices. Top hotels, invitations, champagne, flowers, limousines; hugely enjoyable and habit-forming, and transparently depending upon success.

Arthur Hornblow Jr, a very good friend who twenty years earlier had given me a job at Goldwyn's, now asked me to fly on a highly secret mission to New York. His friend Mike Todd was experimenting with a new hush-hush screen process called Cinerama and felt the need for an evaluation, which Arthur thought I could provide. Besides the plane ticket, Todd was sending five hundred dollars in cash for three days' expenses, a very generous amount in those days.

Mike Todd turned out to be an extraordinary Rabelaisian character, truly something out of a story book. His motto was 'I may be broke but I'll never be poor.' He was a millionaire one day and flat broke the next, a gambler, full of panache, incredibly caring and generous to his friends, showering them with thoughtful and ingenious gifts – he gave the first pocket-size transistor radio to Renée – full of all kinds of schemes and wild ideas and a ferocious joy of life and appetite for adventure. He was also a bandit, cunning and quite ruthless. He lived in tremendous style, had lots of lady friends, later married Elizabeth Taylor and finally died when his private plane crashed in a storm over New Mexico, having taken off against his pilot's warnings.

Cinerama, established on a secluded, very posh Long Island estate, was an intriguing proposition. In a blacked-out indoor tennis court there were three huge screens sewn together and three projectors – one for each screen – creating an enormous panorama of

On location in Arizona.
(Photo: Dennis
Stock/Magnum)

Mike Todd and Professor O'Brien, the inventor of the Todd-AO 'fish-eye' lens.

Oscar Hammerstein at the exact moment of telling me that the company had temporarily run out of money.

Niagara Falls. It was a spectacular visual feast only faintly marred by the seams in between. The total novelty of it was intended to help in the fight against the ominous spread of television which was then causing sleepless nights in Hollywood.

We spent three days in discussion: Todd was a genial host and on leaving I returned three hundred and fifty left-over dollars to him. This caused him considerable worry as he could not bring himself to believe that I had no ulterior motives. For several months he kept asking himself, 'I wonder what kind of an angle he has got?'

No sooner had Cinerama surfaced and become an instant success than Todd had a big fight with his partners and quit, with the solemn promise that he would ruin the new bonanza by making it all 'come out one hole instead of three', and that is exactly what he did. He managed to find a famous scientist in Buffalo, Professor O'Brien of the American Optical Company, who designed a colossal panoramic 'fish-eye' lens for him; this gave birth to the Todd-AO process, and to a deal with Richard Rodgers and Oscar Hammerstein ('R & H'), who wanted to film *Oklahoma!* in the new medium. Joseph Schenck, quite old, and the delightful George Skouras – both shrewd, experienced and powerful showmen – were involved in the financing. Todd and Arthur Hornblow proposed me as the

director: R & H seemed pleased with the prospect and I was eager to accept. The idea of exploring new avenues of movie making was most exciting. Besides, I was enormously fond of *Oklahoma!* and of the radiant optimism and joy of life it had projected during the gray days of World War Two. My enthusiasm was so great that I agreed, without first asking Abe Lastfogel, to a much smaller salary than I should have accepted.

To quote a witty colleague, the story revolved around the question of 'whether a cowboy would or would not take a farm girl to a country dance'. The possibility of taking a Broadway musical and relocating it in the wide-open spaces of the great West, of filming Agnes de Mille's dance numbers in natural outdoor surroundings, seemed too good to be true. Of course there were hundreds of pioneering problems to be overcome before shooting could start; there was only one 'fish-eye' lens in existence, and although more had been ordered and the delivery date guaranteed, we would have to start production with just that one lens and nothing at all to back it up. This caused considerable scratching of heads, and in the end, for protection, it was decided to shoot, simultaneously, a second negative in Cinemascope – in fact to photograph every single scene twice!

Naturally, we had to make extensive tests of the lens and of a specially designed camera, using for the first time the huge seventy-millimeter film, each frame

Above: *The main sets were built in Arizona, as there were too many oil wells in Oklahoma.*

Right: *Gordon McRae and Shirley Jones.*

looking like a postcard. The tests were shot in Hollywood, but in order to see the rushes, we had to *fly* from Los Angeles to Buffalo every time, as there were no laboratories anywhere else where seventy-millimeter film could be developed and printed; all that machinery had been specially designed and manufactured. There were no jet planes then, and those trips took forever. It was great fun and very exciting.

Challenge number two: location trips proved that it was not feasible to film *Oklahoma!* in Oklahoma, where too many oil wells were marring the landscape; instead, we were able to find the most wonderful, soul-stirring location in Arizona, in the San Rafael Valley near the Mexican border, where Pancho Villa's raiding parties had spread terror forty years before. The big set – Aunt Ella's farm – was to be built there. The railroad station for the Kansas City number was already in existence at Elgin and only needed to be re-dressed.

Challenge number three: making the green corn grow to the height 'of an elephant's eye', wildly out of season, in order to accommodate our schedule. Incredible as it seems, the agricultural department of the University of Arizona managed to make this possible, and the ten-foot-high green corn was planted exactly where we needed it.

After four or five flights to and from Buffalo, it was clear that the camera, lens and equipment worked well; meanwhile the all-important job of casting had got under way. Arthur Hornblow, the producer, and I had a veto in the choice of actors, but final approval was in the hands of Dick Rodgers and Oscar Hammerstein. Oscar was particularly impressive: a man of great serenity and warmth and a marvelous writer. Other interesting and attractive people were assembled: Agnes de Mille, a wonderful quicksilver personality, whose job it would be to re-stage most of her brilliant dance numbers in the open landscape; Oliver Smith, an inspired stage designer; and my old friend Bob Surtees, a caustic wit, to photograph this immense spectacle. Art Black, who had always worked with Frank Capra, was not only a great assistant director; he also owned and rented, to film companies, a fleet of highly mobile location toilets, called 'honey wagons'. He was generally known as 'the Shithouse King'.

Gordon McRae.

Shirley Jones.

Above: *Gloria Grahame and Shirley Jones.*
Right: *Charlotte Greenwood.*

Top: *With Eddie Albert, Rod Steiger, Shirley Jones, Gordon McRae and Charlotte Greenwood.*

Left: *The 'fish-eye' lens. Gene Nelson and Richard Rodgers are on the left; I am standing between my assistants, Art Black and Bill Faralla.*

Right: *With Richard Rodgers.*

Above left: *Art Black, first assistant director – 'the Shithouse King'.*

Above right: *Gene Nelson rehearsing the 'Kansas City' number.*

Left: *Agnes de Mille and I were not having a fight – only concentrating on the job. Working with her was a huge delight.*

Finale.

To everyone's delight, a charming young girl – Shirley Jones – was set for the leading part of Laurie; she was found by John Fearnley, an R & H talent scout, in the chorus of one of the *Oklahoma!* companies playing all over America. Hers was a clear, beautiful voice and she blossomed into stardom in a few short years.

For the part of Curly, the cowboy, many promising young actors were discussed and sometimes tested. An excellent singing voice was unfortunately a must, and this excluded some extremely talented young people such as the up-and-coming Paul Newman and a new-comer no one had heard of before. His name was James Dean and Renée spotted him in a TV show. She was very impressed and thought I should meet him; a date was made for us to meet at the super-posh Hotel Pierre at eleven the next day.

Eleven o'clock came and went but there was no trace of James Dean. Finally, forty-five minutes later, he appeared, in battered old cowboy clothes; ruffled, furious and out of breath. He had come into the lobby promptly at eleven and had immediately been thrown out – this was 1954 and second-rate cowboys were not tolerated in grand New York hotel lobbies. After a lot of maneuvering he had finally managed to get aboard a service elevator and there he was.

Dean made a sensational test with Rod Steiger in the 'Poor Jud Is Dead' number. His singing voice may not have been equal to the task, but that test was a classic. I wish I knew if it still lies hidden somewhere in some attic or garage, or whether it has been destroyed. In the end, Gordon McRae, already a star on the New York stage, got the part. He had an excellent presence and a

The ballet.

Rod Steiger and his crew.

Waiting for the next customer.

glowing, warm baritone voice which was most effective.

There was no opposition to my choice of Rod Steiger as the sinister hired man, Jud. I was seduced by his brilliant talent into exploring the character's underlying motives rather than playing him as the straight, despicable musical villain whom everyone loves to hiss. As a result he emerged as a disturbed, isolated person shunned by everyone, and this seduced the audience into a kind of reluctant pity; perhaps unconsciously they felt sorry for Jud, and when he died the jubilation of the community was not echoed by relief in the audience.

There were many other delightful actors in the cast: Charlotte Greenwood, Gene Nelson, Eddie Albert, James Whitmore and, of course, Gloria Grahame.

Eventually we were ready to shoot, and the company – or rather the battalion – arrived in Nogales, Arizona, for a remarkable stay. It was almost like a traveling circus – generators, lights, wardrobe trucks, make-up vans, lots of cars for actors – only the wild

animals were missing. In order to get to the location one had to drive across a stretch of desert criss-crossed by *arroyos*, deep ditches carved out by sudden flash floods – walls of water six-foot high that came roaring out of nowhere in the wake of almost daily thunderstorms. These started around 10.00 a.m. as a few lovely white clouds on the horizon, and gradually built up into enormous thunderheads. By 2.00 the entire sky was an ominous shade of black, and then all hell broke loose – sizzling flashes of lightning, rolling thunderclaps sounding like heavy artillery, and solid walls of water coming down. Cattle were often killed by lightning on the open range, and their bodies would lie there untouched by scavengers who shun anything struck by lightning. Our second unit director, James Havens, was hit as he leant against the hood of a car; the bolt went right through him and shook him up but, miraculously, left him unhurt. One of the heavy passenger cars full of people was caught crossing an *arroyo* and was carried for almost fifty yards by the flash flood. That particular ditch was afterwards known as 'Cadillac Gulch'.

Tim, a marvelous son and friend, then and now.

By five o'clock calm had returned together with brilliantly clear and soft afternoon sunlight – a bonanza for the cameraman. Some of his best shots were made in that light. In the evening a few of our cowboys would stray across the Mexican border and get into drunken brawls. They were, of course, arrested and had to be rescued from the 'hoosegow' (jail) and brought, bleary-eyed, back to work.

When it comes to strangers on the set, film crews tend to be stand-offish, especially if the visitors are wives of the producer or director. There is perhaps a lingering suspicion that they might give an unwelcome report to their husbands. This did not happen in the case of Renée, who had joined me on the Arizona location. Having been a working girl and crew member herself, she was automatically accepted by the crew as one of them. Tim, now fourteen, joined us during his school holidays, spending most of his time with the cowboys. To his huge enjoyment, he rode with them in many actual scenes.

There was nothing extraordinary to report in the production's progress. It all went more or less to schedule. Shooting two negatives made the show enormously expensive but in the end it proved to be a worthwhile insurance as there are very few places today equipped to show the enormous Todd-AO process. Mike Todd used it to great advantage when he made his famous *Around the World in Eighty Days* with David Niven, Cantinflas and Shirley Maclaine – playing, of all things, an Indian princess waiting to be burnt alive. (Obviously she was rescued in the nick of time.)

John Fearnley (Hammerstein's assistant), Arthur Hornblow Jr (producer) and Oscar Hammerstein.

Oklahoma! was intended to be a large spectacle. The film is, of course, at its best when shown in the Todd-AO process for which it was created; unhappily, the facilities for screening it in that manner are hardly available. It is at its second best in Cinemascope. But when seen on a tiny television screen it loses an enormous amount of its appeal, except for the indestructible music. It is truly shameful to see how the opening of the film has been chopped to accommodate an overture.

It remains as one of the most joyful and untroubled experiences in my own memory, the starting point of many lifelong friendships.

A Hatful of Rain
(1956)

It is a curious thing: very often, when making an especially grim picture, all the crew and actors feel a great need to laugh a lot between set-ups – a very natural reaction. Although *A Hatful of Rain* was the grimmest of all the films I ever made, hilarity on the set never, never let up except during rehearsals and shooting. It may be difficult to put this crazy feeling down in writing, but I can try.

We were returning from Havana after the harrowing experience of trying to film *The Old Man and the Sea*, Hemingway's great story which, to me, was about the triumph of man's spirit over enormous physical power, personified by a frail old fisherman and an immense fish locked in a battle for existence. The story's greatness seemed to lie in the deep respect the contestants had for each other, and in their nobility in accepting that they must live up to their pre-ordained fate.

To dramatize the odds I wanted the old man to look weatherbeaten, just leathery skin and bones, and to seem bereft of all strength. Spencer Tracy liked the idea; he agreed gradually to lose a lot of weight during the six months before the start of shooting. The fish – a black marlin – was to weigh a thousand pounds or more; Hemingway knew of a spot off the coast of Peru where they could be found. Alas, things did not work out that way.

Havana Airport, 1955. Hemingway on his way to Capo Blanco, Peru, in hopes of filming a giant black marlin.

Marlin not co-operating; no film. The fading message on the photo reads: 'For Freddie and Renée, one small, edible, non-rubber fish. With love from Papa.'

Top: *Don Murray, Lloyd Nolan and Tony Franciosa.*

Right: *Don Murray looking for a fix.*

Don Murray – withdrawal symptoms.

fish in a studio tank pretending to be the Gulf Stream with an actor pretending to be a fisherman.

Warners behaved extremely well when I resigned; but I hurt the feelings of many people, especially the producer, Leland Hayward, a friend and a splendid man.

The first stop on the retreat from Havana was New York and the Hotel Pierre; I will never forget how happy we were to be there at last. After the blow-up with Warner Brothers, with only Hemingway and Leland Hayward on my side, I was convinced that future jobs would be few and far between.

The phone rang early the next morning. There was an enquiry from Darryl Zanuck at Fox: would I be interested in directing a picture based on a novel by ... Hemingway! – *The Sun Also Rises*? I couldn't resist a hollow laugh; but I just wasn't ready.

Abe Lastfogel kept reminding me gently that a pilot who has been in a plane crash should fly again as quickly as possible, and when Buddy Adler, my old friend from the MGM Shorts Department and *From Here to Eternity*, rang and told me about a Broadway play he had just bought, and which I had seen, I agreed very quickly to direct it. Buddy was then chief of the Twentieth Century-Fox Studios. The play was *A Hatful of Rain* by Michael Gazzo, an uneven, powerful, deeply upsetting work with four fascinating characters and excellent dialogue.

The story, set in New York in the mid-1950s, dealt with a young ex-soldier, painfully wounded during the Korean War and treated with morphine, now a civilian again and a heroin addict – leading a double life, torn between efforts to get his 'fix' and to keep the truth from his family. It showed the effect this had on his young wife, his brother and father.

At that time the drug situation in New York was not totally out of control. Police enforced the law against addicts who were regarded as law-breakers and near-criminals, as well as against the pushers. If caught in the act the addicts were arrested, taken to corrective institutions and usually subjected to 'cold-turkey' treatment – the immediate, total withdrawal of drugs, bringing horrendous pain with it. The cured addict often had no choice but to return to his old haunts and friends

In Peru, Hemingway found the marlins to be camera-shy and behaving in a totally unpredictable way. As a result a miraculous dummy had to be constructed at the Warner Brothers studio; it had a motor inside and could wiggle its fins and tail. It was so big that it had to be shipped – on two railroad flat cars – from Burbank to Miami. Hemingway hated it at first sight and christened it 'the condomatic fish'. When it was put in the Gulf Stream near Havana it sank without trace and was never seen again. Shooting most of the movie in the studio tank seemed to be the only way out; unfortunately, I could not see how this could be done. Meanwhile Tracy had arrived in Havana, not having lost one ounce of weight. Suddenly the story seemed pointless. It made little sense to proceed with a robot pretending to be a

Don Murray and Eva Marie Saint (playing his wife) waiting for the police to arrest him.

and within days he was back on drugs, again leading a sneaky, risky secret life.

US experts declared this law-enforcement policy would backfire and lead to more crime. They cited Great Britain where one could be registered as an addict and where one was thereupon free to buy the 'fix' at a chemist. (In June 1955, in all of Great Britain there were only about 360 registered addicts – 66 of them on heroin.) Films on the subject had been forbidden by the Motion Picture Code, but Otto Preminger's *The Man with the Golden Arm* had been successfully released without the censor's seal of approval. Since then the code had been revised and ours was the first picture made under the new rules.

The first draft of the screenplay was unfortunately rather shapeless, and a replacement for the author, Mike Gazzo, had to be found. The abominable blacklist of the McCarthy days was still going strong, causing some of the best writers to live abroad, Carl Foreman among them. He was now living in London, and when I rang him he agreed to a meeting in Mexico. He and I spent a few days in discussion and shortly afterwards Adler and I received an excellent script from London. In addition to Gazzo's vivid dialogue, it now also had a firm dramatic structure.

The cast was marvelous. Don Murray, grossly under-rated, with an enormous range from tragedy to comedy (Joshua Logan's *Bus Stop*), was a deeply disturbing –

New York, 1956. Skyline, as it will never be seen again.

and accusing – figure, utterly alone in the freezing night as he wandered around the city, desperately trying to find a 'connection'. Tony Franciosa, the brother, had played his part on the Broadway stage; his performance had a shattering intensity; Eva Marie Saint, fresh from her triumph in *On the Waterfront*, was vulnerable and heartbreaking in her confusion; Lloyd Nolan as the father, obtuse and forlorn: all trying to find out what curse had descended upon them – all were very special.

Long before we started shooting, Don and I went through a good deal of initiation and research; he was looking for specific details for the character he was going to play – appearance, movements and general behavior – and I needed to have knowledge of the countless overall aspects of New York's drug scene. We had co-operation from the Narcotics Squad and were taken into 'hot' areas in daytime and in the dead of night, able to observe many things and make mental notes which would be of enormous value to us later on. It was, of course, illegal to prescribe hard drugs to addicts: nevertheless we found doctors who did so and were willing to discuss it. A most harrowing experience was seeing patients at the corrective hospital on Ryker's Island underneath Queensborough Bridge in the middle of the East River, where the hard cases were treated.

The picture was shot in black-and-white, as harshness

was to be a very important part of the film's style. There was a bleak, visual poetry about it. As the brilliant cameraman, Joe MacDonald, had an enormous sense of humor, there was a constant roar of belly-laughs. There was just one drawback: the Twentieth Century-Fox Studios owned the very unfortunate Cinemascope process (I think it was bought by the chairman, Spyros Skouras), and any picture emanating from the studio had to be shot in this ridiculous format, shaped like an elongated band-aid. It tended to defeat the director in his choice of the precise point he wanted the audience to look at; instead, the viewers' eyes went roaming over those acres of screen. It was very rare to see the process used creatively (as in Kazan's *East of Eden*). More often it inhibited one's ideas. I remember spending much time inventing large foreground pieces to hide at least one-third of the screen.

Spyros Skouras, a canny self-made man, had a certain primitive charm about him. He once invited Krushchev (who as head of the USSR was visiting America) to a banquet at the studio and made a well-meant speech before the assembled *crème de la crème*, praising the United States and closing with: 'I was a poor Greek peasant boy when I came to this country; I worked very hard and here I am, the head of Twentieth Century-Fox!' To which Krushchev is supposed to have replied, 'I, too, was a poor peasant boy; I, too, worked very hard and here I am, the head of the Soviet Union!'

Anyway, our production went along well, and after three weeks of shooting interiors in Hollywood we moved East, into the rain, slush and snow of New York's mid-winter. Photographically, these exterior

The cameraman, Joe MacDonald, laughing his head off.

scenes were, of course, very exciting and effective, even though uncomfortable to shoot, and the harsh winter weather gave them an eerie kind of beauty. These scenes have preserved a New York City which no longer exists and can never be seen again – streets and houses are different, the skyline has gone, perspectives and dimensions have disappeared – and there may be a nostalgic value in looking at parts of that movie if a Cinemascope adapter can be found.

Bernard Herrmann wrote a moody score for *A Hatful of Rain*. As expected, the film was powerful, with stunning performances. The only trouble was that very few people went to see it.

To my enormous regret we had to leave Tim – now sixteen years old – as a boarding student in a school which we later found he detested.

The Nun's Story
(1957–1959)

Mike Todd had wanted me to direct *War and Peace*, once *Oklahoma!* was finished. To go from a state-size musical to a continent-size epic was characteristic of the way Mike's mind worked: not long afterwards he produced *Around the World in Eighty Days*. He would have made the first space film if he had lived long enough. Mike's suggestion that Audrey Hepburn should play the part of Natasha made things even more exciting.

Unfortunately Dino De Laurentiis thought so too; he was getting started on his own version, and before our writer, the great Robert Sherwood, had got very far in adapting Tolstoy to the screen we heard that Dino had offered the part of André to Mel Ferrer, who was then Audrey's husband. This meant that Audrey was automatically set to play Natasha in the De Laurentiis film. As it seemed quite impractical to get involved in that sort of race, I resigned from the project. Mike was shattered; his heart was set on that picture. He had been courting Marshal Tito and already two Yugoslav

The nun's family home; Bruges, Belgium, 1957. The brilliant dramatist Bob Anderson agreed to write the screenplay.

cavalry divisions had been earmarked to work with us.

However, Audrey Hepburn and I did find ourselves making a film together a couple of years later. It came about in this way. During the mid-1950s, Kathryn Hulme's novel *The Nun's Story*, based on the true story of a missionary nun who after seventeen years had left her order, caused quite a stir. Miss Hulme had been the chief of a UNRRA camp for displaced persons in post-war Germany and the ex-nun had wound up as a nurse in the same place. They became close friends and Kathryn eventually wrote the bestselling book about her. The theme was stated by Hillel two thousand years ago: 'If I am not myself, who will be for me? And if I am for myself alone, what am I? And if not now, when?'

The book had been sent to me by Gary Cooper who thought that I might find it interesting. He was right. I became engrossed in the idea of dramatizing this woman's enormous problem of conscience. Unhappily, my enthusiasm was not shared by any of the studios. The official word was 'Who wants to see a documentary

Audrey Hepburn.

about how to become a nun?' That summed it up; but when Audrey Hepburn said she wanted to do it the studios suddenly became intensely interested.

With the exception of Ingrid Bergman there was at that time no star as incandescent as Audrey. She was shy, coltish and intelligent; she looked delicate, but there was a hint of iron in the jawline that signified a stubborn will. I thought she would be ideal; and so, now, did everyone else.

The Catholic Church was rather more cautious than the enthusiastic Jack Warner, whose studio now undertook to finance the film. Two things about the project worried them. One was the fact that a professed nun would leave her order after seventeen years – it was not good for recruiting, as one Monsignor put it. The other problem was that we might be tempted to exploit the implicit attraction between the nun and the worldly, cynical, charming Dr Fortunati (played by Peter Finch) whom she assists in the Belgian Congo. The Church did not turn us down flat; they were always polite but

Ghent, Belgium. A corridor in the Convent of La Byloke. (An identical set was built by Alex Trauner in Rome.)

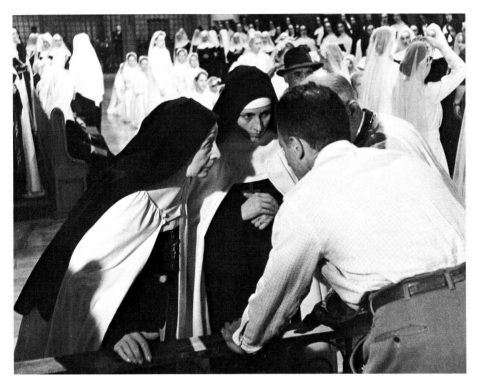

Left: *Edith Evans and Rosalie Crutchley.*

Below & right: *Rehearsal at vestition ceremony, headed by Mother Superior (Edith Evans) and assistant (Renée Bartlett).*

enormously reserved. The first task, then, was to establish our good faith as convincingly as possible.

All film companies approaching the Catholic Church for assistance are put in touch with the Cinema Office which assigns someone – often a Dominican priest – to work with them. The Dominican Order is the order of preachers and as such it is strong on dogma and not particularly flexible. In our case they were extremely thorough in scrutinizing our shooting script. They went through it line by line and objected, for instance, to a speech by Edith Evans: 'The life of a nun is a life against nature.' Our advisers said, 'You mustn't say that. You have to say "... a life *above* nature ..."' More than two hours were spent in discussion of that one word. I remember saying that I'd always thought religious life was a struggle and one couldn't get above nature by simply putting on a habit. We went back and forth without making progress until a Jesuit friend heard about it. He said, 'Why can't you say "*in many ways*, it's a life *against* nature"?' and so, with the Jesuitical addition of 'in many ways', into the screenplay it went.

Finally the approval was given. The production would be based in Rome, with locations in Stanleyville, in what was then the Belgian Congo. This meant that we would be away from home for at least eighteen months, breaking contact with Tim who was now a student at Kenyon College. Ours had been a close-knit family; this was the beginning of a long, worrying separation while Renée and I had a lovely time in Africa, Australia and Europe, with only brief intervals at home.

The real story had happened in Belgium, in Ghent, in a large order of missionary nuns devoted to teaching and nursing. The colony they were posted to was, of course, the enormous Belgian Congo, today's Zaire; so a lot of the work had to do with tropical medicine. That order did not want to know about us; it feared that the film would rake up a scandal well within the memory of many of its members. In the early days, when we asked to see the interior of one of the convents, all we would be shown – very politely – was a printing press or a workshop: we were not to be admitted to the daily routine, much less to the inner life of convents.

Eventually, and thanks mainly to the efforts made by certain Jesuits and Assumptionists, caution gave way to trust and finally to most generous help without which the film never could have been made. We were granted long discussions with many nuns, covering endless subjects. I remember that most of them seemed to agree on one thing: that of the three vows they all must take – poverty, chastity and obedience – the hardest to keep was the last. Detachment from one's individual will was the most difficult thing of all. This was the great problem

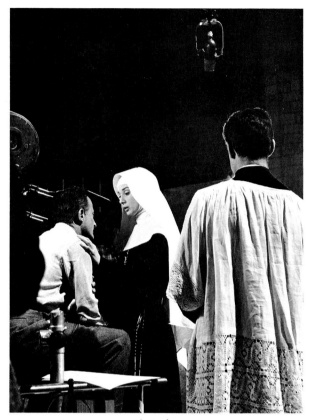

About to shoot a scene with Audrey.

Audrey Hepburn and Renée Bartlett.

for Sister Luke (Audrey) and in the end she lost her fight to achieve that instant, unquestioning obedience. This was the cause of her failure as a nun and of her survival as an independent person.

One of the French religious orders eventually gave us permission to have each of our key actresses stay in a convent for several days, going through the entire ritual of the day starting with the first prayers at 5.30 a.m. I stashed my 'nuns' away at different convents, each one separately, Audrey Hepburn in one convent, Edith Evans in another, Peggy Ashcroft in a third, and so on. Making the daily rounds at 10.00 a.m. to see how they were doing, I'd arrive in the warmth of a taxi (it was mid-January in Paris, the winter was intensely cold and the convents were hardly heated) and all of them would come out of the cloisters absolutely purple with cold but fascinated by what they were involved in and very excited by the way they were getting prepared for their characters.

When you do a film like this you must have, at least, an external appreciation of what religious life is about. If we were making the film today it would have a different feeling; but even when we were shooting it, in 1958, it was already a period piece – beginning in the 1920s and ending during World War Two, with the nun leaving the convent and going off to work in the Belgian Underground – a fairly lengthy time span. The problem of conveying it was complicated by the fact that a nun's habit does not allow much room to show the wearer

Rehearsal in the set built by Trauner (based on the Convent of La Byloke, Ghent).

Above: *Leper colony; Belgian Congo, 1958. Sketch of set by Alex Trauner.*

Left: *The actual set.*

Above left: *Audrey Hepburn at work in a leper colony in the middle of the mile-wide Congo river.*

Above right: *Work photo: Niall MacGinnis plays a missionary-doctor.*

Right: *An actual leper village.*

A leprosy patient.

Dr Stanley Browne, a famous leprosy specialist and head of
a Baptist mission in the Congo.

getting older: so little of her is visible. In retrospect I
can see that this is where I slipped up: in the end,
when Audrey takes off her nun's habit, the passage of
seventeen years of her life is not clearly enough suggested; it is as if time had stood still. Hardly a strand
of gray hair when she shakes it free from the confining
wimple. (There used to be, among hairdressers and
make-up people, an automatic reflex to make the leading
lady look beautiful, come hell or high water, hurricane
or snowstorm, according to a hallowed tradition started
by the founding fathers of the industry.)

Before shooting the Belgian location scenes in Bruges
and going to the Congo, we moved into the Centro
Sperimentale and Cinecittà Studios in Rome, where
Alexander Trauner had designed a most realistic
convent and chapel with convincing replicas of statues
in Bruges, including an early Michelangelo 'Pietà'. It
would have been difficult to distinguish it from the
priceless original. We chose to do the interior photography in Rome so as to be near the Vatican and Santa
Sabina, the Mother House of the Dominican Order who
would continue as our advisers. With their help we
undertook months of research and this turned out to
be an interior voyage of discovery and an enormous
personal experience.

Rome held another advantage. As it was understood
that real nuns were not to be photographed, we needed
to find extras for the large complicated ceremonial
scenes of walking in procession, kneeling, bowing, and
prostrating themselves – and doing it all more or less
on cue; these women had to have special training. In
the end, twenty dancers were borrowed from the ballet
corps of the Rome Opera and were drilled by two
Dominican nuns, one of them a university professor.
For the nuns' close-ups, faces of great character and
personality were needed. We found them mostly among
the embassies and the Roman 'black' aristocracy: a lot
of principessas and contessas would turn up in their
Rolls-Royces or Mercedes at five in the morning.
Dressed as nuns they looked marvelous. What some
earned they donated to charity.

A tall nun was needed to play the assistant to Edith
Evans, the Mother Superior, and to match her height.
In the end my wife seemed to be the best choice; besides,

she had been in a convent school for years. She agreed and went to get her costume. Returning to the set after lunch I saw a tall nun whom I didn't recognize, smiling at me. It turned out to be none other than Renée.

Otherwise, I preferred not to use Roman Catholics in creative situations. It seemed important to keep an objective approach to the work, without the emotional involvement a faithful believer would bring to it, as this would create a private sentimental quality I wanted to avoid at all costs. Our writer, the playwright Robert Anderson, was a Protestant. Edith Evans and Audrey Hepburn were Christian Scientists; Peggy Ashcroft, who was an agnostic, projected a mystic quality to the amazement of the church people, who said she might have been a Mother Superior for many years. Edith Evans made an interesting comment that illustrated how she prepared for her part. She said that she took the character of the Reverend Mother from a line in the book: 'Her back never touched the back of the chair in which she was sitting.' She held herself absolutely straight to show the gap between the chair's back and her own. She built the whole character from that one phrase; it reminded me of the description of Prewitt at the start of the novel *From Here to Eternity* as being 'deceptively slim'. That was Monty Clift absolutely: once I had read

Peggy Ashcroft.

Audrey – lunch.

that description I could never see anyone else in that part.

Looking at the film again, after more than twenty-five years, I am struck by the fine, firm line of development in Audrey's performance. The subconscious quality of independence is present in all her actions. When she comes running in late for the Service her haste betrays the inner calm she should be developing. Or the time when the girls are admitted as postulants and prostrate themselves on the floor in front of the Mother General, Audrey peeks out of one eye, curiosity getting the better of her. Her performance is put together out of dozens of moments of independence, such as the medical exam she is asked to fail in order to prove her humility.

Audrey particularly liked the work of Franz Planer, my Austrian compatriot who had photographed her in

Life around Stanleyville.

These ladies were mad about Chuck Hansen, our unit manager.

Sleeping sickness.

Rehearsing with Audrey Hepburn in the leper colony.
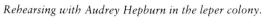

Dr Fortunati, played by Peter Finch.

Peter Finch with Audrey.

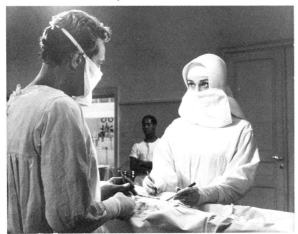

earlier films. Alberto De Rossi, her make-up man, had helped to create the Hepburn 'look' by bringing out the best in her features. Grazia, her hairdresser, was also part of her customary team and in fact played the role of the nun who cuts off Audrey's hair. The hair was actually a wig and Grazia's professional touch avoided clumsiness and fumbling which might have marred that scene.

I have never seen anyone more disciplined, more gracious or more dedicated to her work than Audrey. There was no ego, no asking for extra favors; there was the greatest consideration for her co-workers. The only thing she requested in the Congo, where the temperature hovered around ninety-five degrees and the humidity was incredible, was an air-conditioner. It was promptly sent from the studio in Burbank but did not seem to do much good. On closer inspection it turned out to be a humidifier!

Of course, no conscious physical love affair between the doctor and the nun was to be implied or hinted at; but Peter Finch had the appeal to make the audiences feel the powerful attraction that existed between them. He was not well known at the time but I had seen him in *A Town Like Alice* and had sensed his enormous potential.

I still have one major regret concerning *The Nun's Story*. I dearly wanted to shoot the European parts in black-and-white and only then, when Sister Luke arrives in the Belgian Congo, to burst out into all the hot, vivid, stirring colors of Central Africa. Jack Warner vetoed it: he thought it was too tricky and too far ahead of popular imagination (and popular box office). It would have added greatly to the contrast between austerity on one hand and the explosive fertility and joy of life on the other. We did our best to compensate by shooting the European sequences in muted color; the black and white vestments were of some help.

All this happened in 1958, before the dawn of the jet age. Our journey to the Belgian Congo was long and tiring; it took fourteen hours to get from London to Stanleyville, where we were based. Except for the occasional snakes in unexpected places, such as under breakfast tables, we lived quite comfortably in the Sabena Guest House on food flown in from Brussels

Preparing for a scene with Audrey.

twice a week. Our 'nuns' carried make-up cases and smoked cigarettes between set-ups; the blacks who came to watch the shooting could not believe their eyes. Then someone said, 'Of course these are American nuns.' And the blacks said, '. . . ah, yes, now we understand.'

A promising sequence in our script was planned to show three men who, during a heavy rainstorm, were going to find themselves caught in quicksand and cut off from the banks of a raging, rapidly rising river. People lining the water's edge were to watch, helpless, as the men slowly disappeared in the sand and mud.

A good river was soon found, but the set – a tiny man-made island with three built-in lifts to show the men slowly sinking out of sight – would cost $40,000 to build. In 1958 this was a staggering sum; Jack Warner, the head of the studio, wouldn't hear of giving his OK. Finally, my friend Henry Blanke, one of the finest producers I have ever worked with, had to fly with me all the way from the Congo to Hollywood, in order to persuade Warner of the enormous excitement of this scene. An adventurous showman and a gambler at heart, Jack finally agreed.

On the day before shooting we rehearsed the entire sequence, complete with lifts, wind machines and rain-birds. It all worked to perfection. But during the night the river fell by two feet; all the chicken-wire and cement holding together the 'quicksand' was glaringly exposed. Unfortunately, no one knew why the river had shrunk so suddenly or when it might rise again.

The scene was never shot.

Enormous help was given to us during the entire Congo location by the missionary order of the Assumptionista. The Belgians' colonial policy seemed to be that the natives, even those who were 'evolved', were not yet mature enough to take full responsibility; hence they could be good mechanics but not engineers, nurses but not doctors, sergeants but not officers. We were of course aware of racial tensions in the town. There was a curfew for the blacks, who were not allowed in the European area after sunset. Little did we know that Patrice Lumumba was at that time a post-office clerk in Stanleyville; who could have guessed that

The camera boat.

only one year later the revolution would take place and the Belgians would be driven out.

For four days we worked in a real leper colony situated on an island in the midst of the Congo river, fifteen miles downstream from Stanleyville, traveling there in a small river steamer. Julien Derode, our French production manager, organized a champagne lunch; as we chugged down the immense river dozens of hippos raised their heads out of the water to give us the once-over.

The leper colony was run along the lines of a military outpost by a famous British missionary doctor, Stanley Browne, a Baptist. Naturally, we asked him about the

risks involved. 'You have less risk of getting leprosy here than catching a cold in the New York subway,' he said. After we had finished shooting he added, 'Of course you have to understand that the incubation period for leprosy is seventeen years.'

On the first day everyone was wearing gloves and overcoats; but then we relaxed and found these lovely people most co-operative. Dr Browne was using the new sulfone drugs to stop, though not cure, the ravages of leprosy at the point it had reached on a person's body. Each year they were able to release a small number of people who were declared safe and were returned to their villages after a most moving ceremony which

ended with everyone singing an anthem in their own language: English, French, Lingala and Swahili. The tune was the chorale from Beethoven's Ninth Symphony.

When we were ready to return to Stanleyville, jungle drums were sounded in order to summon a boat; it was just like hailing a taxi. I have never forgotten those drums; they set my own diaphragm vibrating as I stood in front of them.

Franz Waxman composed the score for the film. What I didn't know was that he had a strong dislike of the Catholic Church. When we listened to his music it sounded like the background for the dungeons of *The Count of Monte Cristo*. I decided not to use very much of it. Franz was outraged and complained to Jack Warner. The wrangle centered on my wish to have absolute silence at the end of the film as the nun changes into her civilian clothes and walks out of the convent door, down the back entrance, turning the corner into the main street and quietly disappearing. The conversation went more or less like this: 'Why don't you want music at the end?' Warner asked. I answered, 'Why do *you* want music at the end?' 'Because every Warner Brothers picture has music at the end,' replied Jack. I said, 'If you have festive music you are saying to the audience, "Warner Brothers congratulate the nun on quitting the convent." Is that what you want? If the music is heavy the audience will be depressed; I don't see how you can win.' Audrey was allowed to make her exit in silence.

Above left and right: *Rehearsing the 'quicksand set', with built-in elevators.*

Below: *A bridge in the jungle.*

Farewell at Stanleyville Airport, 1958. Many of these missionaries were killed the following year.

A farewell conga line for us.

With Henry Blanke, our charming producer.

At the London première, July 1959, with Audrey Hepburn, Peggy Ashcroft and Laurence Olivier.

It seems strange to recall now, but to say that Warners were not entirely happy with the film would be an understatement. They thought it would flop. Well, they said, maybe Audrey will bring some people in. It was to open at Radio City Music Hall, a huge, cavernous theater. There was a custom in those days for the general manager to give a cocktail party for the makers of the incoming film. Ours felt like a wake until somebody happened to look out of the window and said, 'Look, there's a long line outside!' The mood changed instantly.

The film cost around three and a half million dollars, a large sum of money in those days. It has recouped it many times over. A local wit suggested a change of title: 'I Kicked My Habit'.

The reaction of the Church was by and large surprisingly good. There was even a very strong positive review on the official Vatican radio station. Of course, many religious groups disliked the film. Some felt it was antiquated and that things were not done like that any more, which is quite true: the film is a period piece of the late 1920s. Others said we had captured many details but that the essence of the religious experience had eluded us.

But although it is a story of a woman who loses the way to her vocation, the strongest memory I retain is the total faith of so many nuns we met and the marvelous serenity with which they went about their duties and devotions: in the middle of the Ituri rain forest, hobnobbing with pygmy friends of our guide, Father Cleuren, we came upon three nuns whose jeep had stalled. They belonged to a French missionary order, living under the most primitive conditions in the steaming forest and charged with providing medical care for the pygmies in the area. There was no question in their minds about ever going back to Europe. In the midst of the infernal heat all three looked as though they had just stepped out of a band-box, starched and shiny; except that one nun's sunglasses were cracked.

One of the hospitals nursing the terminal leper cases was run by an elderly Dutch nun who had been there for thirty-five years. She exemplified all the joy of life even though she spent her days among people who were dying. I asked her if she had ever been back to Europe. She looked at me in amazement: 'Why should I go back? I have never been sick.' That was the only possible reason that occurred to her. Such serenity, fastness of purpose and devotion were awesome qualities for an outsider to witness, especially for a movie director.

One year later very many of these extraordinary people were dead – killed in the revolution that ended Belgian rule in the Congo.

The Sundowners
(1960)

It is helpful for a director to be an optimist with a strong instinct for gambling and for taking chances. A crisis should be regarded not as a problem but as a challenge. This was very much on my mind when I became involved in directing sheep the following year. It all came about in this way:

While filming *Oklahoma!* we often talked about future plans. Oscar Hammerstein's wife, Dorothy, who comes from Tasmania, would urge me to make a picture in Australia, which at that time was virgin territory for films. No one in Hollywood would go near it, and, except for Harry Watt's *Overlanders*, and *A Town Like Alice*, hardly any internationally-known picture had ever been made there. A very small film industry existed, with excellent technicians; the films themselves were mostly documentaries. It was understood that Dorothy would send me books she thought interesting, and over the next few years she did. Eventually, in 1958, she sent me a novel by Jon Cleary, *The Sundowners*, a high-spirited love story of a migrant sheep-drover and his wife of fifteen years, who make their living by herding mobs of sheep from one forlorn place to another. Owning nothing but the clothes on their backs, an old horse, a broken-down cart and a tent, they feel totally secure as long as they have each other. He loves leading the life of a nomad, moving from one sheep station to the next, gambling and boozing; her back is hurting, she wants to settle down and get an education for their fourteen-year-old son. There is also a 'kelpie', a dog to keep the sheep in line. The novel is full of humor, warmth and lovely Aussie ('Strine') dialogue.

Jack Warner was ready and willing to go ahead with the picture. A first draft was written by a young client of the William Morris Agency, one Aaron Spelling. Unfortunately it was not satisfactory; thereupon a reputable writer, Isobel Lennart, was signed and did a good,

Sheep-drovers, South Australia, 1960.

if sentimental, version; part of the trouble was that the dialogue was not Australian enough. Eventually Jon Cleary himself solved these problems and the time came to discuss the budget and production.

The first challenge soon presented itself: the studio quite naturally assumed that the whole thing could be shot close to home; Arizona could easily double for the outback. There are plenty of eucalyptus groves in California; there would be no problem finding kangaroos and emus. It all seemed simple enough and, from the studio's point of view, logical and right. There was consternation when it turned out that I wanted to shoot in Australia. Jack Warner, who, after *The Nun's Story*, had said 'Never argue with success', was nevertheless suspicious that this was a whim; pointing out that the logistics alone of moving actors and crew halfway around the globe would cost an extra half-million dollars, he asked to hear my reasons.

It is a pleasure to say that, as a showman, he under-

Bob Mitchum.

Deborah Kerr.

stood them very quickly. The story was not about landscapes but about people: were we to shoot in Arizona it would emerge as a half-assed Western with bars instead of pubs, cowboys instead of sheep-drovers – they move differently, walk and react differently. Unlike in the old West, no one carried guns in the outback. How could we reproduce the Aussie atmosphere on American locations? Warner did not need a computer to be convinced. He agreed that the film would follow the production pattern of *The Nun's Story*; it would be based in London and the interiors would be shot there at the studios in Borehamwood.

Before long we moved to London, leaving Tim on his own for yet another year and a half. An excellent British production staff was assembled, with John Palmer as production manager, Peter Bolton as my assistant, 'handsome' Jack Hildyard as cameraman, the inseparable Elizabeth Haffenden and Joan Bridge – known to the crew as 'the bookends' – for costumes, and, of

Above: *The drover's mobile home.*
Below: *Sketches by Russell Drysdale.*

Glynis Johns, civilian, and ...

... in character as hotel-keeper.

Peter Ustinov playing a remittance man in Australian exile.

course, Gerry Blattner as the Warner Brothers ambassador-at-large.

Casting came next: Deborah Kerr and Robert Mitchum for the couple, young Mickey Anderson as their boy, Peter Ustinov as a 'second-son' remittance man, and Glynis Johns as a hotel-keeper in the outback. In addition, there was Sam, a lovely, thirty-year-old white horse, to pull the cart; he had once won a beauty contest as the most handsome milk-horse in Sydney. During the production he fell deeply in love with Lola, a flirty young mare who teased him and drove him wild. It broke his heart when we had to move Lola away in the end. We also had a famous ten-year-old Australian racehorse, Silver Shadow, who had broken a number of records and was retired after a heart attack; a true champion, now being ridden by champion jockey Neville Sellwood (who died a year later in a racing accident), doubling for Mickey Anderson.

Ustinov had a problem with horses. He was scared

of them and they of him, and the moment he got in the saddle he would forget all his lines. Peter used to keep us in stitches. Once he told a hilarious story about himself playing a prince of Prussia in a small-budget film when every minute counted – the producer was very nervous about the budget, the director very temperamental. On a dark gray day in mid-winter Peter had to review a parade while seated on a white charger. Not knowing that this was in fact a circus horse, he pulled on the reins just as the dragoons were thundering past; his mount, reacting to a familiar cue, knelt down on its

forelegs at the most majestic moment. What made the story unforgettable was the fact that Peter played every character in it: himself, the horse, the producer and the director.

It is too bad that most of Bob Mitchum's remarks and jokes are unprintable. He is one of the wittiest and most respectful men I have ever met – very allergic to people who take themselves seriously. Bob had a colorful way of expressing himself; if, for instance, he had to go to the toilet, he would say, 'I've got to drain my lizard.' His Australian accent was perfect; he had the

Other actors.

Above: *A crown fire is threatening.*

Left: *Mitchum and the sheep-shearers.*

Actual shearers at work.

uncanny knack of making any accent sound as though he had been born with it. In fact, he didn't get along with the Aussies very well. He felt victimized and outraged by the blunt possessiveness of the local fans and autograph-hunters. His great problem was the shearing; especially the lifting of a four-hundred-pound Merino sheep. As

the entire fleece has to come off in one piece, he was terrified of cutting off a nipple or a vein running close to the surface under the sheep's left jaw; this would make the sheep bleed to death. He was unable to do the job without first having several bottles of beer. On the other hand, he had great fun fighting in a free-for-all

Twenty-four hours on a rough location.

Young Mickey Anderson with Sam, a thirty-year-old gelding who once won a prize as the best-looking milk-horse in Sydney. On our location he fell desperately in love with a flirtatious young mare named Lola.

between two mobs of sheep-shearers at a temperature of 108 degrees, in the middle of nowhere. What amazed him was that the Aussies kept breaking each others' ribs even after I had said 'Cut'. They simply couldn't stop, they were having so much fun.

There were many interesting actors – Australian, British and American, and, of course, Deborah and Glynis, wonderful actresses, who were delightful company. There was the great Chips Rafferty, an Australian idol, playing a station foreman. The British crew were excellent, apart from their irritating habit of calling union meetings on my time in the midst of shooting. This did not seem very sporting, to say the least, but I was powerless to stop it.

Real sheep-shearers were mingled in with actors in certain scenes – brawls, shearing, gambling and

pub-crawling. They acquitted themselves nobly, by just being their usual selves. Three or four shearers came back to London with us and immediately went 'English': bowler hats, stiff collars and rolled umbrellas.

Last, but not least, were the sheep. If not a problem, they were certainly a challenge: On the first day of filming, there was a simple shot of 1,500 sheep (which Warner Brothers had bought for the film and later sold at a profit) walking past the cameras on the trek to an outback station. The leading sheep came to within twenty yards of us, stopped dead and refused to move, in spite of urgent invitations by drovers and dogs. The other 1,499 sheep just walked in circles round their leader. We were awash with sheep; we couldn't make them budge, nor could we get them to back up. We had to lead all 1,500 of them in a wide circle back to where they had started and the whole day was lost. But we got even with them the next day: everyone wore dark clothes and hid behind hastily erected hedges. Leading the procession, there was now one tame sheep on a long leash. There was also a recording of bleating lambs; then the tame sheep (which had not been shorn) fainted because of the heat and lay on the ground, flat as a rug. It was soon revived and we got the shot, but I learned that not

Hands-on directing.

only must a director have empathy with his actors: when directing sheep he must have empathy with them as well; he must learn to think like a sheep.

One of the assignments of our excellent second unit, headed by Lex Halliday, with Skeets Kelly as cameraman and young Nick Roeg as his assistant, was to get shots of a bush fire – a frequent and devastating occurrence in Australia. As soon as the next one was signaled, the unit flew near the spot, hired a taxi and started shooting.

The crown fire is an Australian specialty. It moves along at enormous speed, jumping along the *tops* of exploding eucalyptus trees and scattering their burning fragments far and wide like projectiles. As the unit kept filming, the air grew hot. Suddenly, the fire had switched direction and was coming at them at thirty miles an hour. On scrambling back into the taxi they found the motor had stalled. It is a miracle they managed to get out alive.

The promotion of the film, unhappily, was not a success. The campaign settled heavily on misleading information, perhaps on the guess that the reawakening of Deborah's sexy image in *From Here to Eternity* would bring in the customers. In posters and ads the love story was played down and the impression given that she was a highly-sexed lady who could hardly wait for the *sun* to go *down* so that she could lay her hands on Bob.

After brief initial success at New York's Radio City Music Hall, the final results showed that the sex customers were disappointed and the rest of the public mostly stayed away – a sobering experience, as there was much that was good in the picture, including some of Dmitri Tiomkin's music based on lovely Aussie sheep-shearing and convict songs.

Oposite, top left: *The famous director Nick Roeg, then a camera assistant to Skeets Kelly, and much prettier than he is today.*

Opposite, top right: *'Her Majesty', the script girl Elaine Schreyeck.*

Opposite, bottom left: *Jon Cleary, author of the novel, co-author of the screenplay and a lifelong friend, playing a bit part.*

Opposite, bottom right: *Bob and Deborah decide to laugh at disaster.*

About to direct a bush race in deepest Australia.

Renée reading news from home.

Behold a Pale Horse
(1963)

Two years went by, marked by an unsuccessful effort to make a movie from James Michener's novel *Hawaii*. There was a great deal of script work and some fascinating research in Norway and in the South Pacific, but things did not work out, and a year later I found myself looking for other stories. After a while a slim volume with the curious title *To Kill a Mouse on Sunday* arrived, sent by Mike Frankovich, the chief of Columbia's overseas productions. It was written by the eminent Emeric Pressburger and was set in Spain, several years after Franco's 1939 victory, ending the Civil War that had divided the country in utmost bitterness and hatred. That conflict had been a turning point in world history, the dress rehearsal for World War Two; the moment, signposted by Picasso's *Guernica*, when civilization began its slow relapse into barbarism and the New Dark Ages. A worldwide outcry was raised when, for the first time in history, a civilian population was bombed from the air and an entire town destroyed. Fifty years later, this now seems like an everyday occurrence.

Making a picture on this subject had always seemed important and Pressburger's novel revived my hopes. The story was based on one of the anti-Franco heroes, a man named Zapater, who had escaped to France after the Civil War, lived across the border and made occasional daring and crazy sorties into Spain until he was ambushed and killed. He must have been a very brave man. His friends said he had the heart of a fighting bull; they all felt guilty to be still alive. In the novel he is called Artiguez; his antagonist is Viñolas, a captain in the Guardia Civil, the élite Gendarmerie Corps, who organizes a deadly ambush. Artiguez' mother, dying in her hometown hospital, is the bait. The bad news is delivered by an informer to her son, who immediately decides to visit her; he is about to cross the border into

A messenger from the Spanish underground crossing the French border.

'Death of a Spanish militia man', Robert Capa's famous Civil War photo (1938).

The old leader (Gregory Peck).

Spain when he hears of the trap. Deliberately he accepts the challenge, knowing that it means almost certain death.

He does not see his mother, already dead by the time he arrives. The trap is sprung; choosing to kill the informer, rather than his declared enemy, he himself dies in a hail of bullets.

Tony Quinn had originally wanted to play Artiguez, but I had a feeling that such type-casting could make the film seem literal and predictable. It seemed that we needed someone who could be deceptively gentle, yet capable of ice-cold ferocity. No wonder I was thrilled to hear of Gregory Peck's interest in playing that sort of desperate character. Turning in a riveting performance, he succeeded in hiding the warmth and gentleness that are so much a part of his nature. Tony Quinn, a great actor and a joy to work with, came through with the portrait of a powerful and frightening bully. The rest of the cast were excellent, especially Paolo Stoppa, Raymond Pellegrin and Marietto Angeletti, a sensitive ten-year-old boy who is now a doctor in Italy.

The book had a mechanical feeling about it: it needed a lot of work, but the prospects were exciting. We would have to go to Spain and do all the police research on the spot – and of course this was 1962, when Franco was still very much in power, using the Guardia Civil as an instrument of repression: we had to assume that we would be stopped and questioned. The idea that Viñolas, a captain in that officially sacred institution, would be the villain of the film raised delicate questions, especially for Columbia Pictures: a film on the subject could destroy their company in Spain. (In fact, this is what happened: Columbia was forced to sell its Spanish distribution business. Unofficially, they were quite relieved, as they could make more money by selling each

fell in love with his sets to such an extent that he kept adding details to his studio street for days after we had finished shooting there.) All went well on that trip but there was no doubt that we were closely watched at all times.

An even more important reference for Artiguez would be contacts and meetings with political refugees, mostly anarchists still living precariously on the French side of the border, mainly around Perpignan, many still actively involved with the remnants of the underground movement inside Spain. We needed to see how they lived and

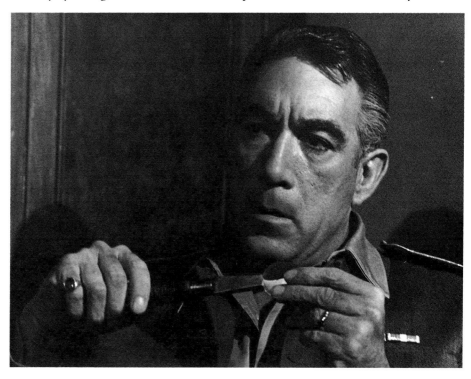

His enemy (Anthony Quinn).

picture outright from then on. They even made a profit from the sale of their facilities.)

Thanks to Mike Frankovich's connections, the Spanish authorities agreed to let me and Trauner, the great Hungarian production designer (also known as '*trop cher*' – too expensive), travel freely through northern Spain. It was important for me to observe how people behaved *vis-à-vis* the gendarmes in what was still a Fascist police state. Also, it was important for Trauner to get details of the buildings to be constructed later in the Paris studio, since there could, of course, be no question of shooting the film in Spain. (Later, Trauner

what they thought and felt after twenty-five years in exile. They couldn't afford to trust outsiders; but we were able to have some very hush-hush meetings that turned out to be instructive. Herewith a few notes I made during that trip in 1963:

'Many Spanish refugees who live in Perpignan want to stay there, where they can still "smell the air of Spain just across the border", even though this means menial work and poverty, and better jobs are available further inland in Toulouse.

'The incredible thing about all these people is their intensity. As soon as they start talking, the years seem

The end of the Spanish Civil War in 1939. Remnants of the Republican forces are disarmed at the French border as they cross into exile.

The messenger (Marietto Angeletti).

The priest (Omar Sharif).

to drop away. It is as though all of their Civil War happened yesterday. It is like the way Southerners used to talk about our Civil War of 120 years ago. Zapater is a legend among all of them.

'One of the men had worked actively with Zapater. During one of their actions a hand grenade which he was to throw at a Guardia Civil got stuck in his sleeve. As a result he has a steel hook which he manipulates very deftly; his right hand is also in very bad shape. He is the most bitter among them, smoldering all the time. He listens intently, but his look is turned completely inward except when he wants to make a point. He then fixes one with his intense black eyes.

'One of them said, "We are always carried away by our emotions. We don't stop to listen to reason, we are victims of our temperament and of our ignorance. We are not civilized. The bourgeois revolution never took place in Spain."

'All the Catalonians have a lot to say about the Church of those days. Obviously there was utter ferocity on both sides. "Religion is one thing, but the Church is something quite different," they say. Even the women feel the same way. Most of them are deeply religious but have never set foot in a church since they arrived in France twenty-five years ago.'

The research for the film had been very exciting; suddenly it was time for the production to begin. The exteriors were shot mostly on the French side of the Basque country around Pau, Lourdes and Gotein, and even on the Spanish border itself, high up in the Pyrenees. Renée described the scene in a round-robin letter to friends:

'One of the most breathtaking (in every sense of the word) locations was the Brèche de Roland. It is something one has to see and feel and be part of. It is about 8,000 feet high, partially a glacier snow-covered the year round, on the border of Spain. There is a monumental gap in the mountain; legend says that it was made by Roland, the medieval hero, who was ambushed here by

The captain's private life.

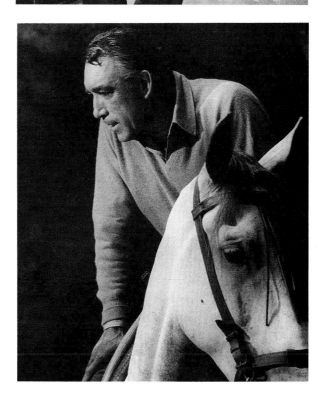

Left: *One of our locations: Gotein, a Basque village in the French Pyrenees. The three steeples stand for the Trinity.*

Below: *Rehearsing near the Basilica of Lourdes.*

Near the shrine of Lourdes. The priest is kidnapped.

the Saracens; before dying he broke his sword against the rock. To us, the breach seemed a visual omen of what was awaiting Artiguez on the return to his country.

'The silence was soon disturbed by the far whining of a plane coming from the direction of Spain. As it got closer, we saw that it was a military plane, hovering over us for a while, circling several times, while our crew stood nervously peering into the sky. Then it disappeared as suddenly as it came and our crew heaved a sigh of relief and went back to their wine and mammoth ham sandwiches. We never come on location without our wine and sandwiches.

'We had some harrowing technical problems while in this Nirvana. The batteries for the camera gave out, someone forgot the proper filter and they ran out of

film. In the midst of all this the clouds began to form and the pilot said he would be leaving in five minutes, otherwise we would have to spend the night and as many days as necessary on top of the mountain. And so in great haste the mountain was evacuated.'

The shrine of Lourdes was another fascinating location involving a sub-plot, a confrontation between Artiguez and a young priest. We were allowed to film near the Basilica by the Bishop himself, a jolly pink-faced man in his late fifties, who told me how to best control my quick temper: by wiggling my toes ten times. (I tried it and it works!) He was bursting with vitality, although a few years earlier he had had a massive heart attack and had been given up by the doctors. Thereupon he decided to make the pilgrimage himself; this was hazardous as it meant immersion in ice-cold water, usually fatal to heart patients. The doctors had no objection as the man was a goner, anyway; but the Bishop's own clergy protested very strongly: 'Imagine the scandal, the Bishop of Lourdes dying of a heart attack in his own pool!' 'Nevertheless I went ahead,' the Bishop told me. 'I won't say it was a miracle but here I am.' 'Why was it not a miracle?' I asked. 'Because it was not

Zapater: an authentic picture of the rebel hero.

instantaneous; it took six months for me to recover.' Many other extraordinary things could be told about this place, where only sixty-four authentic miracles have occurred in the 130 years of its existence.

During location shooting we lived in a rented villa in Pau, complete with a strongly pro-Franco Spanish maid and an elderly French cook, a rabid Communist, who spent most of the day screaming at each other. Most of the crew were new to me except for Trauner, the veteran from *The Nun's Story*, and 'the bookends', Haffenden and Bridge (from *The Sundowners*). The cameraman, Badal, a friend and fellow-Hungarian of Trauner's, was very slow and very stubborn. On occasion I had wish-dreams about putting a match to his beard; but he was able to create an extraordinary mood in his black-and-white photography. A superb job of enhancing the mood was also done by the composer, Maurice Jarre. Back in Paris the sets were built in the small, now extinct Studio St Maurice in Vincennes. (Renée's letter again:)

'Trauner spent months constructing a most beautiful reproduction of a Spanish town. It was perfect in every detail, including the merchandise in the shop windows. Walking down the street one had the eerie sensation of actually being in Franco's country. One of our refugee Spanish extras came up to me in a state of agitation. She said she had seen several Guardia Civils – what were they doing here? Should she make herself scarce? I told her to go over and talk to one of them. She did, and was amazed to find he didn't even speak Spanish. He was a French actor. Her face was a study in incredulity, relief and amusement.

'In one scene we used two Spanish refugees, dressed – much against their will – as Guardia Civils. We gave them sub-machine guns and told them to go to it. No actors could have duplicated the terror and savagery they brought to their roles; they played it to the hilt, with cold and detached deadliness. It is a good thing there were only blanks in the guns.

'Anthony Quinn turned out to be a very interesting and colorful person. He was co-operative and professional and very entertaining. He is mad about his baby and hates to leave it even for a minute. It is quite a sight to see this huge man carrying a tiny little mite only five months old all over the place. He took him to the bull pen and showed him the bulls. He put him on the horse and had his picture taken riding it. He would call to him from the arena and the baby would look at him, his face wreathed in smiles.'

The Spanish border at the Brèche de Roland, high in the Pyrenees. Artiguez (Peck) walking to meet his destiny.

The ambush at the hospital.

The Guardia Civil cheering their leader.

When it was finished the film seemed quite exciting with its haunting music and stylish photography. Frankovich and other Columbia executives had great hopes for it and launched it well. Unfortunately it fell below our expectations – and below the box office returns the company needed to get its money back. Columbia did all it could to promote the film but audiences stayed away. Perhaps we had no right to take it for granted that the general public would identify with the story and develop a rooting interest in those unfamiliar characters. Still, the movie does not seem to have aged, perhaps because the issues continue to be very much alive.

A Man for All Seasons
(1966)

Nineteen sixty-five, the following year, was marked by an abortive attempt at Twentieth Century-Fox to make a film about General Custer and the Sioux Indians. Wendell Mayes' fine script treated the events largely from the Sioux point of view, whereas Zanuck decided that he would rather stick to the traditional image of Custer, the great hero. The budget turned out to be three times as high as the estimate and that was the end of the matter.

Later, I spent a few weeks in Moscow and Leningrad as the US member of the jury at the Film Festival, which was won by Bondarchuk's *War and Peace*. Finally, a

Below: *King Henry VIII (Robert Shaw)*. Right: *Thomas More (Paul Scofield)*.

269.

fascinating effort was made to portray the work of the United Nations' peacekeeping mission on the Kashmir cease-fire line separating India and Pakistan. It was to be produced by Sam Spiegel and I was to direct it, and this led to an extraordinary journey on both sides of the line; first on the Pakistani side, from Rawalpindi up the Indus river valley and on into the Himalayan foothills; and afterwards to India, from Lahore (in Pakistan) to Srinagar and beyond. Sadly, this project also came to nothing.

Back in London I had been in the doldrums for a few weeks when Mike Frankovich phoned: 'Have you seen the new play, *A Man for All Seasons*?' he asked – 'Yes' – 'Would you like to direct the picture?' – 'Yes,' I said.

This was a strong play written by a promising young dramatist, Robert Bolt. It dealt with the sixteenth-century English statesman Thomas More, beheaded on the orders of his king, Henry VIII, for refusing to sanction his marriage to Anne Boleyn. With Paul Scofield in the lead, the play was a powerful emotional experience. It dramatized the nation's unquestioning submission to the absolute power of the King, in stark contrast to More, whose last words before the execution were 'I die the King's good servant, but God's first.'

Bolt, who became a lifetime friend, wrote a first-draft screenplay, one of the finest I had ever read, in less than five weeks. My only regret was that he had cut out a wonderful character, 'Matthew', a sort of one-man Greek chorus whose only ambition was to survive and to 'keep breathing' – the absolute opportunist against the absolute idealist. Matthew was actually more of an abstract principle than a living character and he changed bodies as the play progressed: he was the butler in More's house to begin with, and finally it was he who was the executioner.

With the exception of André Malraux, Bolt is the only writer I have ever encountered who not only did not mind cutting a major character out of his own play or novel, but actually performed the surgery himself. I

Top: *Anne Boleyn (Vanessa Redgrave).*
Left: *Alice More (Wendy Hiller).*

The snow incident: 7.00 a.m.

The same place at 9.30 a.m. after shooting had finished.

bemoaned the loss of Matthew but Bolt said, 'It's a theatrical device, it won't work.' For six weeks we tried to get Matthew back into the script, but it just didn't happen. Bolt was right.

As far as Columbia was concerned this was a very modest and, in a box office sense, totally unpromising project. It had many counts against it: 'Nobody wants to see a costume movie'; very little action, let alone violence; no sex, no overt love story and, most importantly, *no stars*, in fact hardly any actors that the US public had ever heard of. No wonder the budget was tiny and no attention was paid to us by the front office during the shooting – this is of course always a blessing. Mike Frankovich, usually enormously helpful, was snowed under by the production of *Casino Royale*, a very big picture. Fortunately he assigned Bill Graf as executive producer, the man who made it possible for us to open the film in New York just seven months after we had started shooting.

Owing to the extraordinary calibre of the crew and the actors and the way they worked together, this was in every way the easiest film I have ever made. But, in an eerie manner, providence also seemed to take a hand:

The Duke of Norfolk was to ride through a snowy landscape to see the dying Cardinal Wolsey; it was now mid-April and all England was free of snow. Undaunted, Bill Graf and Bill Kirby rented two enormous trucks full of styro-foam (the sort used by airports for fire-fighting) to be spread on the location. Hardly had we arrived

there late in the evening, when, lo and behold, snow started to fall. It snowed all night and at dawn the hills looked sparkling white; the styro-foam trucks stayed where they were. Stranger still, just after we had finished shooting and I had said 'Cut' for the last time, the sun came out and all the snow melted in less than half an hour, as if on cue.

Another incident: in the course of a scene played by Paul Scofield and Robert Shaw (Henry VIII) in More's garden, the King was to grow angry; as he spoke a certain line, a sudden violent gust of wind shook the trees, as if on cue. The sudden wind sprang up each time that particular line was spoken – in long shots, reverse shots, close-ups – and we always had a perfect match in the editing.

We had exactly the kind of weather we wanted all the way through shooting, but on the last day, just when I had finally said, 'It's a wrap,' rain started and fell for weeks afterwards.

Because of the tiny budget, we had to be enormously careful about building sets and making costumes. Fortunately one of the great production designers, John Box, was with us. Using three enormous flats raised in perspective, he built a replica of the palace at Hampton Court for £5,000. When comparing photographs of the movie set and the real thing, no one could tell the difference.

Orson Welles played Wolsey, swathed in scarlet cardinal's robes. John Box had the brilliant idea of putting this huge man in a tiny, cramped office. Welles filled it with his presence until there was no oxygen left to breathe. There was no furniture except a small desk – so visitors would have to stand – and, as the finishing touch, the walls were painted in the same shade of red as Wolsey's robes.

The large courtroom set where More is sentenced to death was conceived by us as a kind of bullring, to convey the feeling that the final outcome had been decided long before the victim entered through a dark, narrow passage.

Finally, the most interesting of all challenges: for the King's visit to More we had to find a tidal river representing the Thames flowing past More's house (in whose day the Thames was a waterway teeming with river traffic, not unlike today's motorways). A wall protecting the house and garden was to be built next to the water. King Henry was to arrive with his courtiers in the Royal barge and impatiently jump overboard too soon, sinking into mud up to his ankles. Furious at first, he suddenly bursts out laughing; his courtiers – the 'yes' men of the period – can do nothing other than jump after him, ruining their pretty finery and laughing at the delightful adventure.

For the mud to be there we needed a tidal river, close enough to the sea for the tide to rise and fall; but by 1966 every single estuary in England was crammed with modern shipping, cranes and modern buildings. Nervous weeks went by until Roy Walker, a young assistant architect, discovered that Lord Montagu of Beaulieu in Hampshire owned the *bottom* of a small river on his estate. For suitable consideration, yachts at anchor were removed and we had two miles of pristine 'Thames' to ourselves, complete with birds and wildlife; the garden wall was built next to it with steps leading to the top.

There is a very old Benedictine Abbey in Oxfordshire, Studley Priory. Secularized by Henry VIII, it is now a charming hotel, ideal for the house of Thomas More,

Cardinal Wolsey (Orson Welles).

Above & below: *We needed a tidal river so that King and courtiers could jump into mud, but every single estuary in England was choked with modern shipping and cranes. In the nick of time the privately-owned Beaulieu river was found.*

Opposite: *Thomas More entering Hampton Court Palace.*

but miles away from any river. It was all there except for the river wall; so, a second wall was built to match the first. The King walked up the flight of steps in Hampshire and descended into the garden a hundred miles away.

The costumes would have cost an enormous amount if they had been in authentic detail. Fortunately our two designers, Elizabeth Haffenden and Joan Bridge, knew how to dispense with all the non-essential frills and to concentrate on the basic outlines of the clothes, using details such as the Chancellor's Chain of Office only when the story demanded it, without distracting the audience's attention from the actual source of the drama: the eyes, faces and hands of the actors.

For the first few days the crew did their usual work very well, the way they would have done on any job, but on

Above: *The trial. More facing Cromwell (Leo McKern).*
Left: *Rehearsing the execution, with Archbishop Cranmer (Cyril Luckham).*

the third day, when Scofield made his speech about the majesty of the law, they were suddenly mesmerized by the magic of those words and they remained that way throughout the rest of the filming. So totally did Paul convey the scope of More's character that for months afterwards I couldn't help but look at him in awe, as a saint rather than an actor.

Robert Shaw, an enormously talented actor whose death was sadly premature, was young Henry VIII, brilliantly projecting the moody quality of the man, his sudden unpredictable lapses from the utmost joy of life

Working with Vanessa and Robert Shaw.

Casting is to a great extent an instinctive, irrational and highly creative process. We were apparently taking an enormous risk in casting John Hurt in the part of Richard Rich, perhaps the most challenging part in the entire play; a young lawyer who starts out as More's dedicated admirer and disciple, is slighted by the great man, turns against him and finally destroys him.

At the time, John Hurt was an unknown young actor who had never played in a film. We were drawing uncomfortably close to the shooting date and still had not found anyone to play the character, until I happened to see John in *Little Malcolm and His Struggle Against the Eunuchs*. I knew he was our man when I saw what explosive nervous energy he was capable of. Time would not permit making a test, so I gambled and cast him regardless. How fortunate we were!

Finally there was Vanessa Redgrave, who did a brief walk-on as Anne Boleyn. Her name is not to be found on the screen credits. She had originally agreed to play More's daughter, Margaret. But then she arrived one

to dark depression coupled with suspicion and persecution-mania, which made him so lethally dangerous.

Then there was Orson Welles, playing Cardinal Wolsey. He had been quite difficult to track down, and when I finally met him, in an apartment in Curzon Street in London, he was sitting behind a magnum of champagne, complaining of liver trouble. He said, 'My French doctor tells me that one must surprise one's liver.' Reluctant at first to play the part, he arrived on the set only superficially acquainted with his lines. Fortunately, his personality and his genius were so immense (and Paul Scofield's patience so enormous) that he succeeded in creating the illusion of absolute self-confidence.

Welles had a marvellous, endearing sense of humor. We were working on a scene with the Duke of Norfolk coming to collect the Chancellor's chain from Wolsey. During rehearsals the 'dying' Cardinal was lying on his cot, puffing the longest, fattest Monte Cristo cigar. We started shooting. Nigel Davenport (the Duke) entered, played his scene and on leaving said, 'Have you a message for the King?' – 'Yes,' said Orson, 'tell him the take is no good – there was a plane in it!'

I had an obsession about having Wendy Hiller play More's wife. She is an extraordinary actress, particularly marvellous at doing a 'slow burn', the slowly growing anger and indignation and failure to understand why More, by refusing to submit to the King's wishes, is placing himself in deadly peril.

Robert Bolt listening to a dialogue problem.

Rehearsing the garden scene with Shaw and Scofield.

day very upset: she had been offered the lead in a new stage play, *The Prime of Miss Jean Brodie*. Could she be released? It seemed impossible to say 'No'. Luckily, we found that the marvelous Susannah York was available and she saved the situation.

However, the next crisis followed promptly: a very brief scene was to be filmed with Anne Boleyn and Henry VIII at their wedding reception. For Anne we needed an actress who, in forty-five seconds, could convince the audience that she was capable of changing the course of an empire. We looked at dozens of ladies, beautiful and/or sexy, but try as we did, we couldn't

Working with Paul Scofield.

immense help and did a splendid job scoring not only *A Man for All Seasons* but *The Day of the Jackal* and *Julia* as well.

When an hour's length of assembled film was shown to the Columbia executives there was a sudden change of atmosphere and a mounting excitement. Frankovich and Bill Graf were beaming, as well they might; they had been wonderful allies all along. Now that it was safe, others came eagerly out of the woodwork to pat me on the back and offer advice – it took me back twenty years to the first studio screening of *The Search*.

An intense campaign of promotion followed and the results were pleasant, producing very good box office and, a few months later, six Oscars.

Renée in 1966.

find anyone who seemed right. Finally, in desperation, I turned to Vanessa, who was now playing Miss Brodie at night and filming all over swinging London in Antonioni's *Blow Up* during the day. 'It's one day's work,' I told her. She immediately agreed, but insisted on two conditions: no screen credit, and no salary.

She and Robert Shaw rehearsed for an hour, and we shot the scene in less than a day. Vanessa did almost nothing except lean forward and blow into her sovereign's ear. She was seductive and totally convincing in showing the magnetism and the power of this woman. The next morning my secretary went to the flower market in Covent Garden and Vanessa's dressing room was full of roses when she arrived for the matinée of *Jean Brodie*.

This was the first time I had worked with Georges Delerue, a brilliant, inventive composer who was of

Man's Fate: A Non-Picture
(1969)

The cancellation of Man's Fate, *a turning point in the film industry's ways of doing business, brought about front-page headlines in Hollywood's trade press. The traditional handshake deal was dead. Lawyers rejoiced.*

There was a long pause after *A Man for All Seasons* – almost three years preparing a picture based on the great novel *Man's Fate* by André Malraux. It was an enormously exciting project; but in the end nothing came of it as the film was cancelled in the midst of rehearsal a few days before we were to start shooting. This is not unusual by today's standards; but in 1969, at the time when this happened, Hollywood people were staggered – not so much by what had been done as by *how* it had been done. The fate of *Man's Fate* marked the end of an era in picture making and the dawn of a new one, when lawyers and accountants began to replace showmen as heads of the studios and when a handshake was a handshake no longer.

The old motion-picture chiefs knew about the irrational side of the business they had created. They loved movies; Sam Goldwyn, producing a film he liked, could say, 'I don't care if it makes a dime, but I want everybody in America to see it.' Irving Thalberg, about to produce *The Crowd* at MGM, would tell the director, King Vidor, 'The studio has made a lot of money, they can afford to make an experimental picture once in a while, it's good for business.' There had been a common language, a common bond; but now the no-nonsense industrial approach took over.

The writing of contracts had always been an endless affair; sometimes they were not signed until *after* the end of shooting. No one was unduly worried about this; in common practice a handshake and a paper called 'Heads of Agreement' meant you had the 'green light' and production could start rolling. But now the contract became the all-important creative effort; cost-efficiency was king.

During the years of pre-production for *Man's Fate*, my contract had never been quite ready; a few 'if's and 'but's had always to be reconsidered. No one, except Chris Mann, my splendid London agent, seemed concerned about it. In the meantime, an excellent screenplay had been written by Han Suyin and locations were found in Singapore and Malaysia. We were now rehearsing with Liv Ullmann, David Niven, Peter Finch and other brilliant actors, in sets dressed and ready to start shooting the following week.

During those three years, a number of expensive MGM pictures had gone over budget and failed at the box office. A new management had taken over; I received warning that several projects might be cancelled. This was soon followed by a legal cable stating that production of *Man's Fate* had been cancelled and the accounts closed; it also meant that henceforth no salaries would be paid. I soon found that no one in the unit wanted to stop rehearsing, salary or no salary; the excitement generated by the story was too strong. We worked for three more days until the script was fully rehearsed, scene by scene. Then, after the usual farewell party as if on the set of a real picture, everybody went home. The next day I went to the front office to see what was going to happen.

The information I received was that MGM had spent more than four million dollars in pre-production. This would be written off; but there were still some bills outstanding. The studio's accounts were now closed; my contract was not signed, therefore I had *no* contract, meaning that it was I who would have to pay those bills.

'How much?' I asked, somewhat stunned.

'A million seven hundred.'

I couldn't believe my ears. 'How do you expect me to pay?'

'It isn't too difficult.' The man gave me an encouraging smile. 'All you have to do is go bankrupt and appoint us as the receivers, then we can make good deals with the creditors.'

'That's dishonorable,' I said.

The man was amazed. 'This has nothing to do with honor, this is business!'

I looked at him and left. The next day I sued the company on behalf of the creditors, including myself. It was an eerie feeling, like walking down a long, empty, windblown street, alone and the wind quite cold. Executives ran for cover, all but two brave men – Paul Mills and Andrew Mitchell – who testified on our behalf. It took four years before we won a victory of sorts but to my regret we did not get the right to influence the settlement of the creditors' claims.

The company's studios were the best equipped in all Britain. They were sold shortly after the cancellation of our film and thereupon ceased to exist.

The Day of the Jackal
(1971)

A year later, during a visit to the distinguished British producer Sir John Woolf, I noticed a fat manuscript on his desk.

'It's a suspense thriller. I just bought it,' said John. 'It will be published next month. You can't put it down.' He was right. I started reading after dinner, finished bleary-eyed the next morning, picked up the phone and asked John, 'Why don't we make this one?' He agreed. The book was Frederick Forsyth's *The Day of the Jackal*.

Freddie Forsyth had been a reporter assigned for several years to cover de Gaulle. With his photographic memory he had assembled a mass of details about the man and, having lost his job after a row with the BBC while reporting the war in Biafra, he sat down and in thirty-five days finished a riveting case history about the 'Jackal', a contract killer hired by conspirators to assassinate the General. The book was a terrific chase, an intriguing mixture of fact and fiction, very visual and full of suspense, even though everyone knew the outcome; as de Gaulle had survived all attempts on his life. To the last moment the reader was kept in the dark as to where and how the attack would take place. The

Above: *De Gaulle*. (Photo courtesy of French Army archives)
Right: *With 'our' de Gaulle.*

Below: *The rifle, capable of being smuggled in small pieces across any border, could be assembled in less than two minutes.*

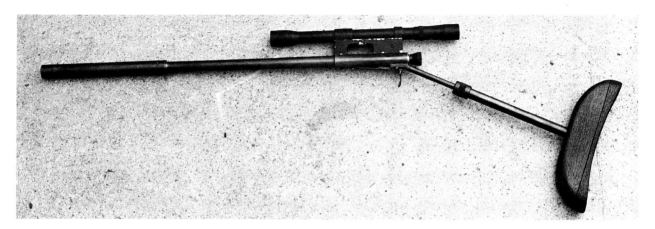

Left: *Place Montparnasse: the actual memorial service in front of the old railway station. A research photo dated 1954.*

Right: *Rebuilding the old station to hide the new skyscraper.*

challenge was to see if we could maintain the same sort of breathless expectancy on the screen. It would be like putting together a giant puzzle, all coldly rational, without any kind of emotion.

I especially liked the strong feeling of irony emerging at the very end of the story – the entire government of France, from the Prime Minister down, the army, police, gendarmes, detectives, looking frantically and in total frustration for one little man with a gun who is too clever for all of them; and the lethal plan going wrong, literally at the last instant, just because de Gaulle suddenly bends down for the ceremonial embrace of a soldier who is very short.

The script was in the hands of Kenneth Ross, an excellent young writer, and our job began with hunting for locations and making contact with the police in Paris, where much of the filming would take place. We expected difficulties because of the nature of the story but due to the masterful diplomacy of our executive producer, Julien Derode, we found instead a surprising eagerness to co-operate. Thanks to him, the French police and other authorities came to like the way they

were portrayed, the systematic and efficient method with which they tracked the 'Jackal'. As a result we were able to shoot in restricted locations, inside the Ministry of the Interior for instance – something no movie company, French or foreign, had ever been permitted to do. This, of course, enraged the French press, and there were loud cries of 'Favoritism for the Anglo-Saxons.'

There was another great concession: we were allowed to film *inside* the police lines guarding the huge 14 July parade down the Champs-Elysées, with gendarmes searching for the 'Jackal' among a million spectators, knowing that he would strike within the next hour. At dawn we began to shoot the gradual massing of troops, artillery and tanks – a vast, powerful force, yet quite unable to protect the Head of State from a killer's single bullet. Against this panorama we staged various small incidents: actor-detectives searching among the crowd, a man reaching inside his coat promptly arrested and hustled away to be frisked, the detectives finding nothing but a cigarette case. The onlookers thought this was 'for real' and protested loudly in the French

fashion. Imagine their resentment when we did the whole thing once more in a second take!

The height of co-operation was reached when the police offered to clear the square facing a railway station, the Place Montparnasse – one of the busiest intersections in Paris – of all traffic for three days and even to divert the seven bus lines crossing the square. It was possible to do this only during the weekend of 15 August, when the city was fairly empty. The 'Jackal's attempt on de Gaulle's life during the brief ceremony was to be filmed there. Naturally, we were eager to accept, even though it rained almost non-stop: fortunately the rain did not register on film.

It would have been wrong to make the film a vehicle for some famous star; I thought the 'Jackal' should be cast with a relatively unknown actor, against type, as indicated in the novel – an attractive upper-class Englishman, young, clean-cut and deceptively cheerful and friendly. By chance, I saw Joe Losey's *The Go-Between* and spotted a young actor delivering an impossible line – 'Nothing is ever a lady's fault' – with such conviction that he made me believe it. I immediately felt that this was my man – Edward Fox. He had everything the part needed: he could look starchy and somewhat inbred, with excellent manners – an unlikely type for a hired killer; he could be unobtrusive and lose himself in a

'Our' ceremony, with real troops.

Above left: *Edward Fox taking aim.*

Right: *'Our' de Gaulle, about to embrace a very short veteran.*

Edward Fox.

Edward Fox testing the rifle.

Demonstrating action to Edward.

Edward in action – note absence of left leg!

crowd; and, best of all, he was hardly known to film audiences; this would help to enhance a feeling of realism.

John was quite happy with the idea; but there was a lot of pressure from Universal – the distributors – to have a 'name' actor play the part, and we were invited to consider other possibilities. Throughout the process, which took many weeks, Edward showed great patience and strength of character, while keeping a stiff upper lip. In the end I was able to say with confidence that he was the best possible choice.

A marvelous make-up job helped the 'Jackal' with the disguises he used to keep ahead of the police and gendarmes. His last appearance was as an elderly bemedalled war veteran hobbling along on a crutch, one leg amputated below the knee. For this scene his leg had to be bent back at a sharp angle and strapped tight to his body; all circulation was cut off. The doctor would allow no more than five minutes for this but in fact Edward was tied up for fifteen minutes at a time, and while the pain must have been excruciating, he never showed it. While he was rehearsing his walk, an elderly lady amputee appeared on two crutches around a corner and engaged her fellow sufferer in a little chat. It was funny in a macabre way, and our French wardrobe ladies, in charge of the strapping-up, were wringing their hands: '*Ah, le pauvre monsieur – comme il souffre!*' (Oh, the poor gentleman, how he suffers!')

Compared with finding our 'Jackal', the casting of de Gaulle was easy, thanks to Julien Derode and our ingenious casting director, Margot Capelier. They found an actor, Adrien Cayla, a specialist in impersonating the General who had been dead for almost two years. The resemblance was close. Cayla had studied the smallest details of behavior and gesture; he knew that de Gaulle's hand never touched the rim of his cap when he saluted. The moment Cayla walked into the office we knew that he was 'it'. As we were shooting all over Paris, this resemblance caused quite a few curious incidents. One scene called for Cayla to be driven to the Arc de Triomphe. When he emerged from his car and started to walk, there was a large gasp from the bystanders and one of them, who was not quite sober,

crossed himself and passed out, convinced that he had seen de Gaulle's ghost.

Thanks to John's casting director, Jenia Reissar, the rest of the cast read like a *Who's Who* of the finest English actors: Alan Badel, Tony Britton, Derek Jacobi, Anton Rodgers, Donald Sinden, Timothy West, and many more. Together with Margot's French contingent – Michel Lonsdale and the lovely Delphine Seyrig among them – they were an exciting group to work with.

A victim – Delphine Seyrig.

The construction of the special rifle was a fascinating job, carried out by one of Britain's best gunsmiths. It had to be extremely lightweight, capable of being dismantled into tiny pieces and reassembled in a matter of seconds, and of being completely disguised while being moved through French customs. Actually a functioning gun, a truly lethal weapon, its construction was based on the calculation that there would be time for only one shot aimed at the victim's head.

In case of sudden panic I like to stay away from everyone until I have worked out a solution.

I wonder if someone would have liked to pull the trigger.

In fact, two rifles were made for the film. One reposes in the Cinémathèque in Paris, the other was handed over to the authorities in London, as agreed. Cyril Cusack did a lovely job as the Italian gunsmith: completely impersonal, detached and engrossed in the engineering problem and not for one instant curious about the victim's identity or the possible consequences of the job.

Ernie Archer did a very fine job designing the few English sets. In France, this was the first of three films I had the great luck to make with a set designer, Willy Holt, who is much too modest for his own good.

Nothing short of being a visual genius, his place is with colleagues at the top of the list.

As in most chase stories there were innumerable locations to be found, in Vienna, Rome, Genoa, the French Riviera, England and Paris; it seemed as though we had used every other street corner in Paris by the time we were through.

The film was made in 1972 – only nineteen years ago – when aerial hijacking and massive organized homicide were still a thing of the future. We felt safe in the belief that governments could cope with terrorism; one can't help but marvel at the speed of collapse of our innocence.

Julia
(1976)

Above: *The* Julia *logo.*

Opposite: *Lillian (Jane Fonda) remembering.*

It is odd how one finds the story for the next picture; or perhaps it is the reverse: how a story finds the person destined to put it on film.

Lillian Hellman had published *Pentimento*, a collection of short stories based on incidents from her own life; among them, 'Julia' – brief, haunting and so gossamer-thin as to be almost transparent. I was strongly moved when I read it, although I must confess it never occurred to me to think of it as material for a movie. It was Richard Roth, a young producer with an extraordinary flair for stories and for casting, who became obsessed by its possibilities. He not only got Alvin Sargent to write a first-draft screenplay, but even persuaded Jane Fonda to play the part of young Lillian.

Almost by accident this first draft was sent to me by Alan Ladd Jr and Jay Kanter, who were then running Twentieth Century-Fox Studios. I found it most exciting. There was an urgent starting date and Sidney Pollack, who was to direct, was not available for many months to come. He graciously agreed to withdraw and we had three months to cast and prepare the complicated production and at the same time to work on the final draft of the screenplay.

Set on Long Island and in Paris, Austria and Nazi Germany in the early 1930s, in about the same period as *The Seventh Cross*, the story deals with the friendship and the extraordinary test of courage of two young American women: Julia, a multi-millionairess, and Lillian, a budding playwright. After a protected childhood, Julia travels to Europe, studies in Oxford and in Vienna and becomes dangerously involved with the Austrian anti-Fascist underground movement. Years later, at a moment of extreme crisis, she sends a message to Lillian, now an enormously successful dramatist and the toast of New York, who is spending a glamorous holiday in Paris. Through an intermediary, Julia asks her friend to smuggle a large sum of money into Nazi Germany. The personal risk is enormous; the decision to go or not to go is up to Lillian alone. She is terrified

but agrees, and this leads to a traumatic train journey to Berlin and to a reunion of the two friends in a café where Julia receives the money. Shortly afterwards World War Two breaks out and Lillian is forced to return to America. In the meantime, Julia has been the victim of a political murder.

Except for a brief meeting in Rome I had not seen Lillian Hellman for about forty years – since 1935 in fact. She liked the script and I believe she liked the picture. She now lived in Martha's Vineyard and because of ill health could not come to London until later. Adored by many, despised by others, Lillian told me that the real 'Julia' was still alive in New York. She would not mention her name, saying vaguely that there

were legal reasons why she preferred not to go into details.

A few years later an autobiography by a Dr Muriel Gardiner, a psychiatrist in her seventies, entitled *I was Mary*, appeared in print. Her story was uncannily similar to Julia's: she was an heiress, had studied in Oxford and with Freud in Vienna, and had been involved with the Austrian underground. The odd thing was that no one remotely resembling Lillian Hellman had ever been a part of Dr Gardiner's life; in fact the two women had never met. Research in Vienna established that there had been *only one* American girl in the movement and that her code name had been 'Mary'. Lillian and I were no longer on speaking terms

Vienna, 1936. The Austrian Fascist militia (Heimwehr) on parade, two years before the Nazi 'invasion'.

by that time; however, she seems to have maintained that Dr Gardiner was *not* 'Julia' and that there had been someone else. It is believed that a man who knew both ladies might have told Lillian the story. The mystery remains – if it is, indeed, a mystery?

Jane Fonda was ready and most eager to start work, and the search was on for 'Julia'. Logically, this part should have been played by an American actress, but movies have very little to do with logic (except for book-keeping, of course). The person who seemed to combine all the essential qualities of style, breeding and an almost mystic dedication – Vanessa Redgrave – is English. Having worked with her ten years earlier, when she played Anne Boleyn in *A Man for All Seasons*, I knew her well. Because of her politics there was strong opposition at the studio to casting her, but she was undoubtedly the right actress for the part and she kept her personal convictions pretty much to herself until a memorable moment at the Academy when, being warmly applauded upon receiving her Oscar, she made a political speech. In thirty seconds the temperature dropped to ice while she, smiling happily, descended the steps, gave me a big kiss and sat down.

Having started life as a cameraman I am strongly oriented toward the visual aspects of storytelling. I like to explain to actors *what I want*, but not *how to do it*, and fortunately I have a clear sense of actors' potential, which allows me to make offbeat choices and to gamble in the casting: and no matter whether the part is large or small, I spend much time discussing it with each of the actors separately, and in depth – the way their character develops and their relationships with other people in the film. In this way we make sure long before the filming starts that we are on the same wavelength; a lot of energy, time and spontaneity is saved during rehearsals and there are few unwelcome surprises later on. I have of course made a great number of wrong decisions over the years.

Top: *Lillian Hellman, 1936.*
Middle: *Dashiell Hammett, Hellman's friend.*
Bottom: *Dashiell, played by Jason Robards.*

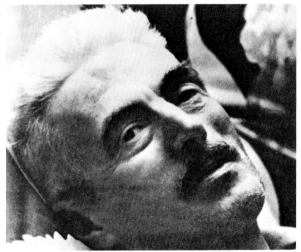

Opposite, top: *Young Julia and young Lillian.*

Opposite, bottom left: *Julia's grandmother (Cathleen Nesbitt).*

Opposite, bottom right: *Young Julia (Lisa Pelikan).*

Above: *St John's College, Oxford.*

Left: *Julia (Vanessa Redgrave).*

Fonda with Meryl Streep (her first screen appearance).

In planning a film one usually develops a vision of how the story should be told – the style of the camera work, the choice of cameraman, production designer, editor, composer and costume designer and, of course, the casting of the right actors and making sure there is strong chemistry between them. It is marvelous if their performances come up to ninety per cent of what one has been hoping for – but sometimes there are actors who give you 120 per cent, who will bring so many unexpected facets to their characters that their work is a constant source of surprise and delight. Vanessa is one of these rare people. Watching her I was sometimes so riveted by her performance that I would forget to say 'Cut' at the end of the scene. She never seemed to be acting; like Spencer Tracy, she was just there.

Jane Fonda did an extraordinary job with her part. She is a splendid actress with a strong analytical mind which sometimes gets in her way, and with an incredible technique and control of emotion; she can cry at will, on cue, mere drops or buckets, as the scene demands. It was fascinating to watch these two women, who come from quite different schools of acting, work together and complement each other so convincingly. I thought Jane well deserved the Oscar she should have got.

There were other important parts: Maximilian Schell generously agreed to play the down-at-heel refugee who is part of the underground network. Max is a

sought-after leading man and it was probably the first time he played a character part. He gave the refugee enormous stature and sympathy and received an Oscar nomination.

The other role was that of Dashiell Hammett, the writer and long-time friend and companion of Lillian Hellman. Jason Robards seemed ideal for the part. Predictably, Miss Hellman objected, but was very pleased with him when she saw the completed picture. After reading the script, Jason was at first not very keen on doing it. 'There is nothing for me to do?' he asked – 'Just say the lines,' I said. He hesitated briefly, but then agreed and later on received an Oscar for his trouble and for his marvelous performance.

There was also a walk-on part, a bitchy friend of Lillian's, played by a newcomer, one Meryl Streep. It was her first film, and she wore a black wig so that now no one ever recognizes her. Watching her, Jane Fonda said, 'This one will go far.'

An eighteen-year-old French actor, Lambert Wilson, had a tiny bit to do on the train. He impressed me so strongly that I cast him, five years later, in one of the

Fonda at Sardi's.

Sardi's restaurant after the New York première of Lillian's first play. The set was built at EMI Studios, London, and actors were brought over from New York.

three leading parts, as the mountain guide in *Five Days One Summer*. He, too, should go far.

There was an interesting problem concerning the style of photography. The best approach seemed to be a documentary one, in black-and-white. On the other hand, we had two great actresses nearing their forties who had to be totally convincing in scenes where they were supposed to be nineteen or twenty; the picture depended on that. To bring this about, a touch of magic was needed, to be supplied by a great portrait-photographer in the tradition of Garbo's cameraman Bill Daniels, or Joe Ruttenberg or George Folsey, someone who knew how to make women look wonderful. (Next to a mountain, a woman is the hardest thing to photograph.) Douggie Slocombe is one of the few

who are left; he photographed Katharine Hepburn, then in her mid-sixties, in George Cukor's *Love Among the Ruins* and made her look absolutely glamorous. Douggie is of course a romantic; he gave our film a lovely warm glow. Although it worked somewhat against the authenticity of the story, I'm confident that, faced with the same problem, I would make the same choice today.

Our production designer, James Callaghan, built a Cape Cod house in greatest detail on a lonely beach in England. As London was our production base it would have been prohibitive to take the entire company across the Atlantic just for that one sequence.

When we moved to France, where about half the film was shot, most of the crew was switched, except for Douggie Slocombe and his three-man gang. The

Left: *Success. Paris, 1934.*

Below: *Success. Versailles, 1934. Identical set by Willy Holt (see the photo of my brother on page 55).*

At the same time (1934) there is an armed uprising in Vienna. The Fascist regime is victorious.

legendary Julien Derode (*The Nun's Story*, *The Day of the Jackal*) continued as executive producer, with Tom Pevsner as associate and with invaluable help from Peter Beale, a young British production executive, who represented the studio. Our brilliant Willy Holt was the production designer in France. Alain Bonnot became first assistant, replacing Tony Waye.

There are two types of assistant director. One is essentially a production man, dedicated to seeing that everything – props, sets, wardrobe – is ready before it is needed, who anticipates all possible and impossible pitfalls, sees that actors are on time and that the schedule is kept; and who is a great diplomat, popular with the crew as well as the director. On location he makes sure that everyone – especially the crew – is properly treated and fed at regular times. Often he rises to an important post in production management. The other kind is a director's assistant, primarily interested in the creative part of the work and not necessarily popular with the crew. One can spot the difference within minutes by the sort of questions they ask. The latter is very imaginative on the set and very good at motivating extras – one of his key jobs – and if the 'chief', looking through a viewfinder for a camera set-up, takes a step backwards

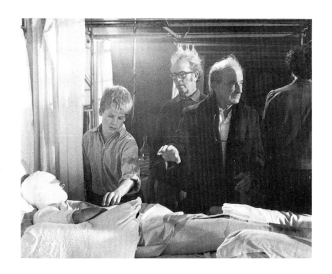

Above left: *Julia, badly wounded in the battle, is fighting for life.*

Above right: *Douggie Slocombe is lighting the 'set', in an ancient disused hospital ward.*

Left: *Julia on crutches.*

Opposite: *'Mr Johann' (Maximilian Schell), an Austrian underground worker* (top left), *asks Lillian to make a dangerous journey* (bottom). *Lillian tries* (top right) *to make up her mind.*

Lillian leaves Paris.

Julia.

Working with Vanessa.
Left: *Julia waiting for Lillian in a Berlin café.*

he will find himself stepping on that assistant's big toe; he's right behind the director trying to see the next scene exactly as the latter sees it.

Having worked abroad with British, French and Italian crews, I have found that they are equally expert at their work, even though their systems and working hours may be different. For the best of them the work is far more than just a job. They become involved in the making of a picture, they respond to the director and are quick to appreciate quality or the lack of it – the French in their cool, analytical way, the Italians with enthusiasm, sometimes breaking into applause for the actors at the end of a scene.

At the original preview in Toronto, we realized that the first ten minutes of the film were not only superfluous but actually confusing and the necessary cuts were made before we opened. Still, there was one more horrendous experience in store for us. It was decided to have the actual opening at eleven o'clock on a Sunday morning – a custom universally accepted by the New York public. The night before there had been a large party in Lillian Hellman's honor, which I didn't attend; there were no executives around when I arrived at the theater just before the first show. I was greeted by a delightful sight: a large SOLD OUT sign above the box office and a long line winding around the corner of the block. My elation didn't last long: David Weitzner, the one and only executive on the spot, appeared out of the packed lobby, white as a sheet and looking as if he had seen a ghost. 'What's the matter?' I asked – 'There's no sound,' he said. 'The sound equipment doesn't work.' All sense of reality faded in a sudden flash; I saw and heard the news but I couldn't grasp it.

The time was 11.05. The house was packed, people were waiting expectantly and beginning to look at their watches. The projectionist was unable to fix his machine and there were no mechanics to be found within miles; it was Sunday morning after all. The theater manager was absent and so was the owner. More phone calls were made and finally a mechanic was found somewhere on Long Island; he could arrive in an hour and a half!

There was only one thing to do: I had to go up on

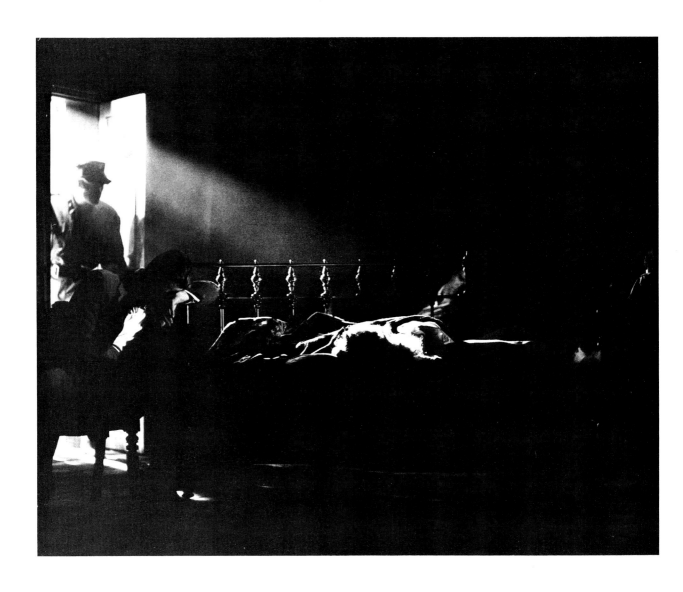

Rehearsal. Fonda slapping John Glover, who asks her really to hit him when filming.

Fonda obliges. John is knocked unconscious.

A director's life is not always easy.

stage, face the public, introduce myself and explain our predicament. In view of the fact that New Yorkers are notoriously impatient and had been waiting for a good half-hour, they were surprisingly friendly and good-natured.

Given three choices – staying put and waiting for almost two hours, or leaving and returning, or getting their money back – a great many stayed, probably because there was a slight drizzle outside.

Things went smoothly once the projector was fixed and the picture did well, with eight Academy Award nominations and three Oscars, including one for Alvin Sargent's screenplay. Curiously enough, the movie was far more successful in Europe, where it touched many witnesses and survivors of that monstrous era.

Opposite, top: *Julia killed by Nazis.*
Opposite, bottom left: *At the same moment, Lillian wakes.*
Opposite, bottom right: *Georges Delerue recording his music.*

Five Days One Summer
(1981)

Once, when asked about my own personal idea of
happiness, I said, 'To sit on top of the Matter-
horn, wondering how the hell I would ever get down.'
It is a dream which will of course remain unfulfilled,
forever.

As a teenager I had managed to climb a few of the tall,
eternally snow-covered peaks in Austria. Unhappily, the
magic was bound to stop when I left Vienna for Paris,
and stop it did for the next thirty years; but, for a
long, long time I dreamt of making a movie about the
mountains of my youth – a movie in which they were
not just a backdrop, but actors with characters of their
own.

It is strange to think that barely sixty years ago – in
my own time – there were hardly enough people to
disturb the majesty of those enormous spaces. There
was elation in being a tiny speck, lost in the brooding,
mysterious landscape; but the greatest thing by far was
the total silence. Each new day brought unpredictable
adventures, small triumphs over sudden panics; in the
evenings, when we rested our aching bones in some
lonely mountain hut, there was a glowing sense of
achievement.

Today, if you are trying to climb Mont Blanc, there
will be fifty people ahead of and above you, dislodging
rocks or sometimes falling past you. Hardly an adventure. Everything is predictable, organized, programmed
and pre-packaged – blaring buses, coach parties in
tennis shoes and stiletto heels, endless noise, empty tin
cans and bits of paper flying about in the wind. I thought
how beautiful it would be to show it all as it once had
been.

After a few false starts, I came across Kay Boyle's
promising short story 'Maiden, Maiden', about a

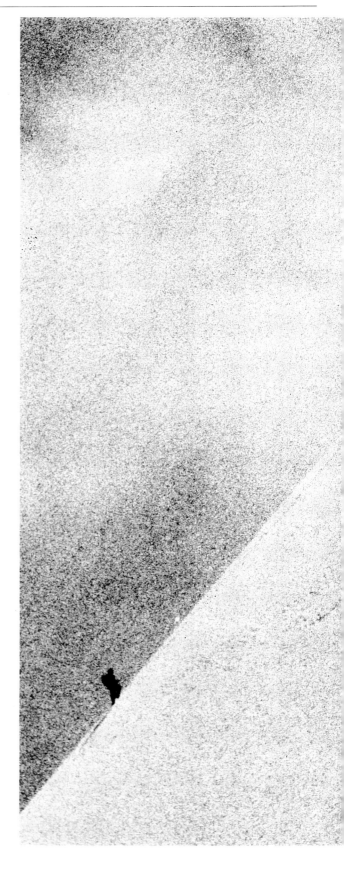

Piz Palü – the East Buttress.

238

Scottish doctor and his young mistress on a holiday in the Alps in 1932. The doctor and his guide are long overdue in returning from a difficult climb. The girl, who has fallen suddenly and passionately in love with the guide, is waiting in a mountain hut below – waiting to tell the doctor that she is leaving him. After many long hours, only one man is seen far in the distance, painfully moving down the glacier. The girl rushes to meet him. Clearly there has been a fatal accident, but until the last moment she – and the audience – have no idea which man has survived.

Alan Ladd Jr and Jay Kanter, producing for Warner Brothers, decided to go ahead with the picture. Sean Connery, eager for respite from the James Bond movies, was interested in playing the lead. Michael Austin was engaged to write the screenplay. He added a remarkable interlude – a centuries-old folk legend about an ancient peasant woman who had lost her bridegroom on the

eve of their wedding. In the fifty years since he was killed in a fall down a deep glacier-crevasse she had never married, never looked at another man.

Even today a number of people die each year, falling into the crevasses camouflaged by thin bridges of snow. Sometimes, many years after the accident, victims' mangled bodies reappear on the glacier's surface, and this happens during our couple's holiday. The body is almost perfectly preserved: as in a time warp, the stooped tiny old woman finds herself face to face with her handsome, seemingly sleeping fiancé to whom she has been faithful all her life.

Willy Holt, who had worked with me on *The Day of the Jackal* and *Julia*, was again the production designer. Young Peter Beale, who had done a splendid job on *Julia*, became the executive producer. Assisted by John Palmer and Tony Waye, this was a first-rate production team. The Piz Palü, part of the Bernina group towering

Above left: *The doctor (Sean Connery).*
Above right: *His girl (Betsy Brantley).*
Right: *The Swiss guide (Lambert Wilson).*

Willy Holt's fake hotel.

above Pontresina near the Swiss-Italian border, was our chosen location.

Mountains are much more difficult to photograph than women; moody and elusive, they don't reveal themselves easily. It takes a very good eye to find their best side; in the wrong light they can look flat and utterly boring. At other times, that same mountain can be dramatic or threatening or deceptively serene. By a great stroke of luck we were able to get Peppino Rotunno, one of the world's great cameramen, famous for his work with Fellini and a sensitive artist in his own right.

Thanks to him and to the mountaineer-cameramen, the visual quality of the movie was lovely and the climbing scenes quite spectacular.

An alpine expert was needed, someone who remembered the 1920s style of climbing and the old, completely different kind of equipment, ropes and clothes. Fortunately Norman Dyhrenfurth, a distinguished Swiss mountaineer and film director, agreed to supervise the details and to direct the more hair-raising climbing scenes.

To work at high altitudes you must be familiar with

lots of small details, otherwise you are inviting disaster. This meant that we had to have a group of world-class climbers with us, who would provide safety for everyone working in dangerous spots, would rig camera positions inside a glacier and in horribly exposed places, above great empty spaces, and work as doubles for the actors in extreme situations. Hamish MacInnes, the chief of the Mountain Rescue Service in Glencoe, Scotland, organized and led that group, which soon became known as the 'Scottish Mafia' – a dozen highly unusual men who are best described as refugees from the twentieth century. All were world-class climbers, some of them famous veterans of Mount Everest, K2, Patagonia, Alaska, China, Russia. A few worked on jobs only long enough to earn money for expeditions to some distant part of the world. Ranging from a self-described plumber (Joe Brown) to a university professor (Paul Nunn), these hard-drinking lusty eccentrics had more fun and more laughs than any group of men I have ever known. When all the liquor had gone at the end of a party in their hotel in Pontresina, they thought it too boring to walk down all those steps from the second floor and instead jumped out of the window. Paul Nunn having forgotten something climbed up the drain-spout and jumped again. This time he split his

Up to no good.

Above: *The chief of the 'Scottish Mafia', Hamish MacInnes, known as 'the Fox of Glencoe'.*

Below: *Joe Brown, the best British climber of the period.*

*To Fred,
Wishing me some
time to climb
next time.
Best wishes,
Joe*

chin, but didn't know it and ran around for three days complaining before the truth dawned. I have never seen such extraordinary contempt for physical pain or danger.

Known as 'the Fox of Glencoe', Hamish organized a two-week mountaineering course for cast and crew, teaching everyone how to move on rocks and steep ice, how to manage ropes, crampons and ice-axes, to watch out for hidden crevasses gaping below snow-bridges and – best of all – how to be winched in and out of helicopters. This was highly enjoyable for three out of ten people: the other seven were scared stiff. It was a feeling of extraordinary elation to be whisked about this colossal landscape, dangling at the end of a piano wire and surrounded by thousands of feet of thin air.

Besides being a genial, delightful gent, Sean Connery was an excellent actor and a good sport. His physical courage and his gruff, sarcastic sense of humor made him enormously popular with the crew. He would much rather have played golf than muck about in mountains, but he didn't grumble when asked to drop, suspended on a rope, into a 200-foot-deep crevasse.

Betsy Brantley, a young newcomer, played the girl. A native of North Carolina, she had studied acting in London and this was her first time before the camera. There was a radiance and a sparkle about her and her natural freshness and exuberance was of immense help.

It was asking a lot, trying to find a young European leading man who would appear credible as Connery's rival, fill the boots of a Swiss mountain guide, project an air of complete authority *and* speak perfect English. After much soul-searching I remembered Lambert Wilson, the teenage boy who five years earlier had played a brief scene with Jane Fonda in *Julia*. As he was appearing on stage in Paris he was not available until the very last moment and had to get his alpine training 'on the job'. Our Swiss guides were not helpful – they resented the idea of having a greenhorn pretending to be the master of a complex craft which needs many years of experience. Fortunately Martin Boysen, one of the leading members of the 'Mafia', took Lambert under

Working at the foot of Piz Palü.

'Scottish Mafia' fixing jump-off point.

Paul Nunn jumping across a 200-foot crevasse – and crashing!

his wing and the young actor came through with flying colors. An excellent supporting cast was headed by Jennifer Hilary, Anna Massey and Sheila Reid.

Willy Holt built the perfect replica of a nineteenth-century hotel, so lifelike that holiday-makers would come in trying to reserve rooms; they became quite confused at the sudden sight of nothing but empty space behind the L-shaped front. (A spot close to the 'hotel' location in the Roseg Valley had been from time immemorial a trysting place for snakes – poisonous adders – which would congregate from all points of the compass, crawling huge distances for their annual mating rituals – a series of incredible gangbangs.) Another of Willy Holt's spectacular achievements was the replica of a primitive, ancient refuge high above the Pers glacier. After we had finished shooting, both sets

were taken down and the locations restored to their pristine beauty.

One of the most important sequences was a scene showing the guide, who suddenly discovers a boot and part of a leg sticking out from the ice wall of a deep crevasse. Hamish had found a beauty of a crack two hundred feet deep. The 'Mafia' built platforms down below and made the whole thing as safe as possible. To solve the problem of the boot and leg sticking out of the ice a hole was hacked in the proper spot, the boot inserted and water poured over the whole thing; frozen, it looked completely natural. It was an awesome experience to be filming at the bottom, in a narrow gap between two shiny vertical walls of sheer ice, in absolute

A 900-foot ice wall at the Porta da Roseg. Note the camera positions on sheer ice. In order to get a better shot, the cameraman asked the climber to 'move over a couple of steps to the right'!

Left: *Auditioning crevasses. We needed one at least 150 feet deep.*

Below: *Hidden crevasses on the glacier: the most dangerous hazard of all.*

unearthly stillness and with only a sliver of blue sky showing far above us; it was like being in a Gothic cathedral, like being present at the beginning of this world. Around noon the rays of the sun would begin to soften the topmost layer of ice, and blocks of different sizes would come whizzing down, forcing us to quit shooting down below and film other scenes in the afternoon. Even so, on one occasion, a camera, knocked over by a flying chunk, fell in my lap. The 'Mafia' claimed I had missed my vocation – I should have been an international goalkeeper.

While we were filming, a real body was found on 'our' glacier; hardly anything was left of it. The only recognizable things were a wallet containing obsolete Swiss banknotes, a wedding ring and 'Vibram' (rubber) shoe soles. Upon tracing the case, it was found to be the body of a Swiss policeman from Lausanne, lost on a skiing holiday thirty-five years earlier.

The music was adequate, but indifferent; it did nothing to enhance the film, I'm sorry to say. Unfortunately, Georges Delerue had not been available. One of the earliest pearls of wisdom emanating from the industry's founding fathers had been: 'Don't make pictures with a lot of ice and snow. People don't want to see ice and snow, they want beaches and palm trees.' I thought times had changed, but I may have been wrong. (Chaplin's *Gold Rush* was, after all, an exceptional masterpiece.) Be that as it may, our film was seen by only a few people when it first appeared in 1982. It vanished rapidly from the world's screens but seems to be emerging again as a minor sort of cult picture. The original title, 'Maiden, Maiden', might have helped, perhaps.

Appendix

Following are the letters, ballot papers and cable referred to in the chapter on *High Noon* (page 97). Please note the instructions at the start of the cable (page 252): 'DLR DON'T FONE' – meaning that the cable *must* be delivered *personally* to each addressee. 'NL' means Night Letter. I seem to remember that the cables were delivered by motorcycle messengers late in the evening.

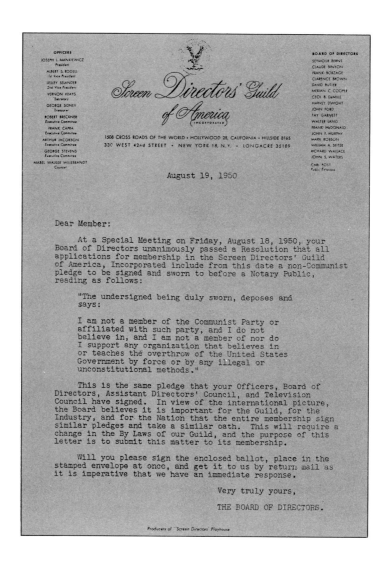

B A L L O T

Approve_____

I, _____
    (Write in your name)   Disapprove_____

an additional Article to the By Laws of the Screen Directors'

Guild of America (Incorporated) as follows:

    All members of the Guild shall execute and
file with the Secretary of the Guild the
following affidavit:

    I am not a member of the Communist Party or
affiliated with such party, and I do not
believe in, and I am not a member of nor do
I support any organization that believes in
or teaches the overthrow of the United States
Government by force or by any illegal or
unconstitutional methods.

    This Article shall become effective upon receipt of a

majority vote by mail pursuant to Paragraph 6, Article IV,

of the By Laws.

Gentlemen:

    I have received, with considerable delay, your letters
of August 19 and 31, regarding the taking of a loyalty oath by the
entire membership of the Screen Directors' Guild.

    Please be advised that I am ready and willing at any time
to take a loyalty oath, provided I am asked to do so by a proper
authority and for sound reasons.

    I am under the impression that the Screen Directors'
Guild is a professional and not a political organization. Therefore
I believe that it is not qualified to administer loyalty oaths
without changing and subverting its entire nature and reason for
existence.

    The Board and the Executive Committee of the Guild are
in essence a group of private individuals. I believe that no such
private group should be permitted to have power and control over
the thoughts and actions of their fellow citizens. Once the first
step has been taken, no one can tell where such procedures would
stop.

    (underneath) Finally and most importantly, I am bitterly opposed to
the method you have adopted in trying to pass this measure. You
have required a signed vote, instead of a secret ballot. This is
a coercive way of voting, adopted in all communistic and other
dictatorships. In this fashion you have attempted to and succeeded
in frightening a majority of the membership into voting for it.
Need I point out the parallel with the "free" elections in Russia
and Nazi Germany?

    Conspiracy against the free expression of thought is a
contemptible thing, regardless of whether it comes from the Left or
the Right. It makes a joke out of voting and makes impossible any
form of loyal opposition. Therefore, it negates and tends to destroy
all democratic procedures.

    At the present time our freedom is threatened from Russia.
We must take proper steps to safeguard ourselves against this threat.
In my opinion, adopting the Russian attitude toward liberty is not
the best way to meet the danger.

    All this should make it abundantly clear to you that I
am not prepared to surrender my individual freedom as a law-abiding
and loyal citizen of the United States of America to any private
pressure group which - for whatever reasons - wishes to subvert
that freedom.

    Sincerely,

    (Fred Zinnemann)

OFFICERS
JOSEPH L. MANKIEWICZ
President
ALBERT S. ROGELL
1st Vice President
LESLEY SELANDER
2nd Vice President
VERNON KEAYS
Secretary
GEORGE SIDNEY
Treasurer
ROBERT BRECKNER
Executive Committee
FRANK CAPRA
Executive Committee
ARTHUR JACOBSON
Executive Committee
GEORGE STEVENS
Executive Committee
MABEL WALKER WILLEBRANDT
Counsel

Screen Directors' Guild
of America
(INCORPORATED)

1508 CROSS ROADS OF THE WORLD · HOLLYWOOD 28, CALIFORNIA · HILLSIDE 8165
330 WEST 42nd STREET · NEW YORK 18, N.Y. · LONGACRE 5-5189

BOARD OF DIRECTORS
SEYMOUR BERNS
CLAUDE BINYON
FRANK BORZAGE
CLARENCE BROWN
DAVID BUTLER
MERIAN C. COOPER
CECIL B. DeMILLE
HARVEY DWIGHT
JOHN FORD
TAY GARNETT
WALTER LANG
FRANK McDONALD
JOHN T. MURPHY
MARK ROBSON
WILLIAM A. SEITER
RICHARD WALLACE
JOHN S. WATERS
CARL POST
Public Relations

August 31, 1950

Dear Member:

The Post Office Department has notified us
that our registered letter containing your
ballot on the non-communist addition to our
By-Laws was received.

Over 80 per cent. of our Guild's membership
has already voted.

Your Board of Directors feels that on this
matter it is imperative that we have a 100
per cent. vote.

Please send in your marked ballot by return
mail.

    THE BOARD OF DIRECTORS

    A. S. Rogell
    _____
    Acting President

ASR:j

Producers of "Screen Directors' Playhouse

TO THE BOARD OF DIRECTORS OF SCREEN DIRECTORS' GUILD OF AMERICA

    Article V, Section C, paragraph 1 of the Screen Directors' Guild of

America By-Laws provides:

    1. Any officer or Director Member of the Board of Directors may
be recalled at any time by the written vote of not less than
60% of the Director membership in good standing filed with the
Board of Directors. The members so voting may, by the same
vote, designate a successor to the person recalled. If no
successor is designated such successor shall be appointed by
the Board.

    Pursuant to the above section of the By-Laws, I, _____,
                                                       (write name)
a Director member of the Screen Directors' Guild of America in good standing,

hereby vote that Joseph Mankiewicz be recalled from the office of President

of Screen Directors' Guild of America.

                        _____
                                (SIGNATURE)

WESTERN UNION

w0A231 LE469

L=WHAO38 NL PD= MVD 1215 ALTA LOMA RD= LOS ANGELES CALIF OCT 13
DLR DONT FONE= [1950]

TRY 34 MALIBU COLONY MALIBU CALIF=

TO ACQUAINT YOU WITH THE REASONS FOR THE BALLOT SENT FOR
RECALL OF THE PRESIDENT OF THE GUILD, WE GIVE YOU THE
FOLLOWING FACTS:

¶ 1= BY OUR BY—LAWS THE MANAGEMENT, DIRECTION AND CONTROL
OF THE AFFAIRS OF THE GUILD ARE VESTED IN THE BOARD OF
DIRECTORS=

¶ 2= THE PRESIDENT SHALL PRESIDE, BUT IN HIS ABSENCE FROM
LOS ANGELES, OR IF HE IS UNABLE TO ACT, THE FIRST VICE
PRESIDENT SHALL ACT=

¶ 3= IN JUNE, MR= MANKIEWICZ LEFT FOR AN EXTENDED TRIP IN
EUROPE= ON FRIDAY, AUGUST 18, WHILE MR= MANKIEWICZ WAS IN
EUROPE, THE BOARD OF DIRECTORS MET, AND AFTER FULL DISCUSSION
DECIDED THAT IN CONFORMITY WITH THE ANTI—COMMUNISTIC BELIEF
OF THE MEMBERS OF SDGA ALL THOSE SEEKING MEMBERSHIP IN THE
GUILD SHOULD BE OBLIGED TO SIGN A NON COMMUNISTIC OATH=

¶ THE APPLICATIONS FOR MEMBERSHIP WERE ACCORDINGLY SO
REVISED, AND UPON ADVICE OF COUNSEL THAT CONDITIONS OF
MEMBERSHIP SHALL BE UNIFORM FOR ALL, THE BOARD UNANIMOUSLY
PASSED A RESOLUTION THAT THE GUILD BY—LAWS SHOULD BE AMENDED
BY REQUIRING TI

SAME OATH OF THE MEMBERS OF THE GUILD=

¶ HOWEVER, THE BOARD DIRECTED THAT BEFORE THE ADOPTION OF
THIS BY—LAW, IT BE REFERRED TO THE INDIVIDUAL MEMBERSHIP OF
THE GUILD= THAT WAS DONE= 618 BALLOTS WERE MAILED, 547
VOTED YES, 14 VOTED NO, AND 57 HAVE NOT SENT BACK THEIR
BALLOTS, BUT OF THIS NUMBER SOME ARE ON LOCATION, OTHERS IN
EUROPE=

¶ 4= JOSEPH MANKIEWICZ ARRIVED FROM EUROPE AFTER ALL THESE
STEPS HAD BEEN ACCOMPLISHED IN A LEGAL AND ORDERLY MANNER=

¶ 5= ON AUGUST 24TH, IN NEW YORK, HE ISSUED A PRESS
STATEMENT CRITICIZING THE ACTION OF THE BOARD OF DIRECTORS
AND THE MEMBERSHIP, WITHOUT FIRST CONSULTING HIM=

¶ 6= THE BOARD OF DIRECTORS IMMEDIATELY HELD A SPECIAL
MEETING AND, BY PHONE, REQUESTED MR MANKIEWICZ TO MAKE NO
FURTHER STATEMENTS UNTIL THE BOARD COULD MEET WITH HIM=

¶ 7= ON SEPTEMBER 5TH, THE BOARD MET AND THE ENTIRE MATTER
WAS EXPLAINED TO MR= MANKIEWICZ, AND THE BY—LAW WAS AGAIN
APPROVED= IT WAS POINTED OUT THAT ANY MEMBER WHO REFUSED TO
COMPLY WITH THE=

THE COMPANY WILL APPRECIATE SUGGESTIONS FROM ITS PATRONS CONCERNING ITS SERVICE

WESTERN UNION

L=WHAO38 LONG 5
(any member who refused to comply with the)
BY—LAWS WOULD NOT BE IN GOOD STANDING, AND THAT UNDER THE
PROVISIONS OF THE EXISTING CONTRACTS WITH PRODUCERS THE
GUILD WAS OBLIGED TO SEND A LIST OF MEMBERS IN GOOD
STANDING AS WELL AS THOSE WHO BECAME NOT IN GOOD STANDING
EITHER FROM NON—PAYMENT OF DUES, OR FOR ANY OTHER REASON=

¶ HOWEVER, THE PRODUCER MAY PAY THE DUES OF A MEMBER NOT
IN GOOD STANDING FOR NON—PAYMENT OF DUES, AND HE MAY
LIKEWISE EMPLOY A MEMBER WHO IS NOT IN GOOD STANDING FOR
ANY OTHER REASON, IF HE CHOOSES TO DO SO=

¶ A MEMBER WHO CHOOSES NOT TO COMPLY WITH THE BY—LAW
REQUIRING A NON—COMMUNIST OATH MAY STILL BE EMPLOYED, BUT
HIS EMPLOYMENT BECOMES A MATTER OF INDIVIDUAL NEGOTIATION
WITH HIS EMPLOYER=

¶ 8= ON OCTOBER 9TH AT THE MEETING OF THE BOARD OF
DIRECTORS, MR= MANKIEWICZ, FROM THE CHAIR, AGAIN OPPOSED
THE BY—LAWS AND CALLED THEM A BLACKLIST= THIS TERM WAS
CHALLENGED BY THE BOARD AS UNTRUE AND INCENDIARY=

¶ 9= THE FOLLOWING DAY AN ARTICLE WAS INSERTED IN VARIETY

WHICH AGAIN SET FORTH THE VIEWS OF MR= MANKIEWICZ AND
REPEATED HIS OPPOSITION TO THE BOARD OF DIRECTORS AND THE
VOTE OF THE MEMBERSHIP=

¶ 10= MR MANKIEWICZ HAS, THEREFORE, PITTED HIMSELF
AGAINST THE LEGAL GOVERNING BODY OF THE GUILD, ITS BOARD
OF DIRECTORS= HE REPUDIATES THE DEMOCRATIC VOTE OF ITS
MEMBERSHIP=

¶ 11= HE STANDS WITH 14 AGAINST 547= THE ISSUE IS WHETHER
MR MANKIEWICZ IS TO RULE THE GUILD=

¶ 12= WE HAVE BEEN WITH THIS GUILD SINCE ITS EARLY
YEARS AND HAVE INVESTED TIME AND DEVOTION TO ITS PRESERVATION
, AND HARMONIOUS GROWTH=

¶ 13= OURS IS A DEMOCRATIC ORGANIZATION= WE RESPECT MR.
MANKIEWICZ'S RIGHT AS A MEMBER TO VOTE "NO" ON THE BY—LAW=
THEN HE, AS A MEMBER OF THE GUILD, WILL HAVE THE SAME RIGHT
AS OTHER MEMBERS TO STAND WITH THE MINORITY OF 14=

¶ 14= HOWEVER, NOW, WE MUST DISAVOW MR MANKIEWICZ'S RIGHT
TO USE HIS OFFICE AS PRESIDENT IN SUCH A DICTATORIAL MANNER
AS TO RENDER THE DEMOCRATIC PROCEDURE OF THE BOARD OF
DIRECTORS IMPOSSIBLE= BY HIS ACTIONS=

HE HAS LEFT US NO ALTERNATIVE BUT TO RECOMMEND THAT HE BE
RECALLED ACCORDING TO THE DEMOCRATIC METHOD PROVIDED IN THE
BY—LAWS, NAMELY, BY YOUR VOTE=

THE COMPANY WILL APPRECIATE SUGGESTIONS FROM ITS PATRONS CONCERNING ITS SERVICE

---

ol. 69   No. 35   Hollywood (28) California, Tuesday, October 24, 1950   13   Ten Cents

MANKIEWICZ WINS; SDG BD. OUT

Postscript

Feeling awkward at ending this book
with an array of pompous platitudes,
I ask your indulgence in finishing
with a photo that speaks for itself.

DOGS MUST
BE CARRIED

Acknowledgements

I beg forgiveness from friends whose names unfortunately are scarcely mentioned in this book: Laslo Benedek, H. E. Reuven Dafni, Phil Kellogg, Rev. Wilfrid Dufault, David Lean, J. Paul Getty Jr KBE, Mrs William Wyler, Dick Widmark, Congressman Robert Mrazek, Joe Mankiewicz, George Sidney, Billy Wilder, Robert Wise, Bob Lennard, Joe Youngerman, Rick Senat, Marvin Meyer, Bob Morgan, John Maeer and Bill Bird. They and the memories of Rouben Mamoulian, Boris Ingster, Hank Potter and Bob McIntyre are in my thoughts and in my deep and abiding affection.

I owe enormous thanks to many people for their generous support, especially to Laura Morris – it is only fair to say that without her constant encouragement there would have been no book; to Gary Kurtz, Stanley Bielecki and Lucie Martin who first persuaded me to write it; Jack Black, a great diplomat who saved me from all sorts of legal pitfalls; Linda Mehr of the Academy of Motion Picture Arts for her immense help on many occasions; David Reynolds for whose patience and courtesy I'm most grateful; Paul Fielding for the excellent design; Jane Thomas; Penny Phillips; Liz Pitman; Roger Davis and Owen Laster; David Savile; Lofty Rice (Pinewood Stills) for his outstanding photographic work; David Meeker of the British Film Institute; Sallie Colak-Antic; Katarina Tana for her splendid help with the mountains of photographs; David Roberts for old times' sake; Margaret Spencer for the pages she endlessly and uncomplainingly re-typed; and last but certainly not least my assistant, Linda Ayton, the Rock of Gibraltar, for finishing that job, and for her dedication and loyalty.

Picture Credits

I would like to express my special gratitude to the Academy of Motion Picture Arts and Sciences, the University of California in Los Angeles (UCLA), the British Film Institute (BFI) and the American Film Institute (AFI); also to the *Guardian* (page 110 *top*), the Imperial War Museum, London (page 93 *bottom*), Yad Vashem, Jerusalem (page 62) and the Wiener Library (pages 60, 61, 222).

Grateful acknowledgement is made for permission to reproduce photographs courtesy of the following:

LOEW'S INCORPORATED, METRO–GOLDWYN–MAYER INCORPORATED: *The Seventh Cross* © 1944, renewed 1971; *The Search* © 1948, renewed 1975; *Act of Violence* © 1948, renewed 1975; *Teresa* © 1951, renewed 1975

REPUBLIC PICTURES CORPORATION: *The Men*; *High Noon*

COLUMBIA PICTURES INCORPORATED: *A Member of the Wedding* © 1953, renewed 1981; *From Here to Eternity* © 1953, renewed 1981; *Behold a Pale Horse* © 1964 Highland-Brentwood Productions; *A Man for All Seasons* © 1966 Highland Films Limited

RODGERS AND HAMMERSTEIN: *Oklahoma!*

TWENTIETH CENTURY-FOX FILM CORPORATION: *A Hatful of Rain* © 1957, renewed 1985; *Julia* © 1977

WARNER BROTHERS PICTURES INCORPORATED: *The Nun's Story* © 1958; *The Sundowners* © 1960; *Five Days One Summer* © 1982

MCA PUBLISHING RIGHTS: *The Day of the Jackal* © Universal Pictures

DEPARTMENT OF FINE ARTS, FEDERAL GOVERNMENT OF MEXICO: *The Wave*

All rights reserved by copyright proprietors

Photographers' Credits

George Sidney: pages 45, 118 *right*. Robert Capa/Magnum: page 186 *top*. André Kertész, courtesy of the French Ministry of Culture: page 15. Ned Scott: *The Wave*. Emil Berna: *The Search*. Harold Zegart: *Teresa*. Schuyler Craig: *High Noon*; *Oklahoma!* Alfredo Valente: *A Member of the Wedding*. Sandy Roth: *The Nun's Story*; *The Sundowners*. A. di Giovanni: *The Nun's Story*. George Higgins: *The Sundowners*. Paul Apotheker: *Behold a Pale Horse*; *The Day of the Jackal*. Norman Hargood: *A Man for All Seasons*. George Whitear: *Julia*. Graham (Noisy) Attwood: *Five Days One Summer*.

Photographs by Fred Zinnemann: pages 18 *top*, 19, 20 *bottom*, 21, 22 *bottom*, 25, 26, 28, 29, 38, 39, 43 *top left*, 76, 78 *bottom*, 85, 179, 207 *bottom*.

All other photographs from the author's collection.

Index

Page numbers in *italic* refer to illustrations